TExES

Special Education Supplemental Practice Questions

Mometrix

TEST PREPARATION

Dear Future Exam Success Story

First of all, **THANK YOU** for purchasing Mometrix study materials!

Second, congratulations! You are one of the few determined test-takers who are committed to doing whatever it takes to excel on your exam. **You have come to the right place.** We developed these practice tests with one goal in mind: to deliver you the best possible approximation of the questions you will see on test day.

Standardized testing is one of the biggest obstacles on your road to success, which only increases the importance of doing well in the high-pressure, high-stakes environment of test day. Your results on this test could have a significant impact on your future, and these practice tests will give you the repetitions you need to build your familiarity and confidence with the test content and format to help you achieve your full potential on test day.

Your success is our success

We would love to hear from you! If you would like to share the story of your exam success or if you have any questions or comments in regard to our products, please contact us at **800-673-8175** or **support@mometrix.com**.

Thanks again for your business and we wish you continued success!

Sincerely,
The Mometrix Test Preparation Team

Printed in the United States of America

Table of Contents

Practice Test #1

1. Carter is a sixth-grade student with an intellectual disability. Why would the use of manipulatives be an appropriate instructional strategy when teaching a math lesson?

a. Manipulatives can stimulate the sense of touch in students with intellectual disabilities.
b. Manipulatives can make math lessons more enjoyable for students with intellectual disabilities.
c. Manipulatives can help students with intellectual disabilities learn classroom rules.
d. Manipulatives can aid in communication for students with intellectual disabilities.

2. Which of the following is most accurate about what teachers need to consider in planning lessons in reading and math for both special needs students and the class as a whole?

a. They already know which skill or concept they want to teach.
b. They assume students have prerequisites for a skill/concept.
c. They must determine what mastery of a skill/concept requires.
d. They are premature in thinking how to expand/apply learning.

3. Rebecca has intellectual disabilities and has lived at home with her parents all her life. She has no job skills. Her parents are getting older and would like her to have a job when she finishes school. She has been placed in a group home and a day habilitation training program. Which scenario is most suitable for her?

a. Attend academic classes in the training center and work in a workshop part time.
b. Receive job training in classes at the training center and transition to a workshop.
c. Be placed in a sheltered workshop immediately instead of in the training center.
d. Learn work skills at the training center and then have a job at the training center.

4. Mr. John and Ms. Deere are team-teaching a special education class of high school students who are deaf or hard of hearing. Mr. John has written a lesson plan of multimodal activities based around a scenario involving a boys' basketball team. Ms. Deere is recommending some changes to this lesson plan as she feels it is biased. Which of the following is the most likely basis for her objections?

a. Mr. John's lesson plan is not likely to be one to which the female students can relate.
b. Mr. John's lesson plan is not likely to appeal to students with hearing impairments.
c. Mr. John's lesson plan did not include any input from Ms. Deere when he wrote it.
d. Mr. John's lesson plan focuses on a physical education activity with no academics.

5. Which of these is not an example of assistive technology (AT) that could be used in assessment?

a. A pencil wrapped with tape
b. A text-to-speech computer
c. A word processing program
d. These are all examples of AT

6. Which time-out strategy is most effective for very young students?

a. None; time-out has been proven ineffective for young students.
b. Warn the student of the consequences before delivering it; make him or her sit silently and alone for a set amount of time; warn him or her that repeated offenses will result in the same consequence; allow him or her to rejoin activity.
c. Make the student sit away from the group, ideally facing away from activity, and then require the child to apologize for his or her actions before rejoining the group; failure to apologize results in longer time spent away from the group.
d. Warn the student of the consequence; if action is repeated, make him or her sit away from the group for a set amount of time; debrief with student about the reasons for the time out; communicate expectation for behavior before rejoining activity.

7. Carly is an elementary school student who uses a wheelchair. Two small plastic parts on her chair have broken, rendering it unusable. Carly is using an uncomfortable "loaner" chair. She is unhappy without her own chair. Carly's parents are having financial difficulties. Carly's teacher sees these things and wants to do something. Which of the following might she do?

a. She finds a charitable group that repairs wheelchairs for free.
b. She does nothing, because this is not her job as a teacher.
c. She pays for the repair herself to help Carly's parents.
d. She finds a charity to donate a new chair to Carly.

8. Which of the following is MOST likely to be a universally applicable lifelong writing skill for eighth-grade students?

a. Email writing
b. Essay writing
c. Letter writing
d. Résumé writing

9. Nina is a student who has severe hearing impairment. She wears a hearing aid and has a low level of hearing. She can communicate verbally but speaks very loudly. Nina visited the public library in the past, but the local librarian was upset at the disruption created by her loud speech. The librarian now does not like Nina and does not want her in the library. What does Nina's special education teacher do?

a. She tells Nina that the school library is just as good and that she should do all her library activities at school instead of aggravating the local librarian and putting up with her rejection.
b. She supervises Nina during visits to the public library and teaches her to control her voice while there; she also helps establish a friendly relationship between Nina and the librarian.
c. She complains to the school principal about the local librarian, saying she is discriminating against Nina because of her disability.
d. She sends Nina to the school psychologist for counseling to console her after her feelings have been hurt by the local librarian's disapproval.

10. The school psychologist can be a crucial member of the Individualized Education Program team. Which responsibility does the psychologist typically hold?

a. Administering IQ tests
b. Administering achievement tests
c. Administering progress monitoring probes
d. Administering transition planning inventories

11. Javier is a fourth-grade student with an emotional disturbance. Which one of the following individuals is LEAST likely to attend IEP meetings?

a. School psychologist
b. Director of special education
c. The student
d. School principal

12. What is an example of a learning objective that is NOT measurable?

a. Students will be able to sound out each letter in the alphabet in six weeks.
b. Students will be able to understand 20% of the English language in six months.
c. Students will be able to complete half of their reading packets in one week.
d. Students will be able to read a chapter of a novel in one day.

13. Ms. Wood is a new teacher. Her first class includes a number of students from urban and impoverished backgrounds. When she gives standardized tests, these students score lower on measures of vocabulary and logic. For example, with word pair completion, given the word "cup" and the choices of "saucer," "table," "fork," or "chair," these students choose "table" rather than "saucer." What is the explanation for this?

a. These students have no experience with a cup and saucer, so a cup sits directly on the table.
b. These students have impaired language development due to poor nutrition and deprivation.
c. These students have never been taught to make logical word associations by their parents.
d. These students do not recognize formal logic because they have never read books at home.

14. Which of the following instructional strategies would be most appropriate in supporting a student with an independent living skills goal of cooking a meal?

a. Allowing the student to help in the cafeteria by cleaning the kitchen
b. Allowing the student to shadow workers at a local restaurant
c. Allowing the student to research ingredients needed to make meals
d. Allowing the student to use the kitchen to cook her lunch each day

15. When working with a general education math teacher, which instructional strategy would be the best in allowing a student with a visual impairment access to the curriculum?

a. Modified assignment length
b. An audio version of the textbook
c. Preferential seating close to the board
d. Extended time on tests

16. Which of the following agencies would likely best help high school students with specific learning disabilities find and maintain jobs?

a. School-to-work agencies
b. Independent living agencies
c. College counseling agencies
d. Military recruiting agencies

17. Which of the following is NOT an example of a graphic organizer?

a. Visual imagery
b. Venn diagram
c. Concept maps
d. Flow chart

18. Which one of the following strategies is likely to be the most beneficial for at-risk students with disabilities who struggle with mental illness?

a. Offering to seek help from the student's parents
b. Asking many detailed questions to seek more information
c. Allowing them to be alone with their feelings
d. Informing the school counselors of the concerns

19. Which of the following is NOT one of the components of a free appropriate public education (FAPE)?

a. All children with disabilities are entitled to FAPE.
b. Schools must provide the best possible education.
c. Schools must notify parents of proposals to change their child's placement.
d. Special education and related services must be provided at public expense.

20. Which of the following strategies would be LEAST effective in structuring an inclusive classroom environment?

a. Providing multisensory approaches to learning
b. Enforcing a rigidly structured routine
c. Developing clear rules and expectations
d. Using station learning opportunities

21. Which one of the following components is most important in attaining goals that are measurable?

a. Concrete evidence
b. Cost analysis
c. Clarified descriptions
d. Overarching objectives

Refer to the following for question 22:

One of Mr. Petrov's high school students struggles significantly with reading comprehension skills. She loses her place often and misreads key words. She doesn't try to correct her errors, even when they make no sense. She can give only a rudimentary summary of what she has read. Based on his observations, Mr. Petrov suspects this student may have a learning disability that requires special education services.

22. Which type of instructional focus would be most beneficial to improve her reading comprehension?

a. Well-organized coaching in decoding, sight words, vocabulary, and comprehension several times a week
b. Weekly instruction on one area of reading; more, and the student will become overwhelmed and likely shut down
c. Instruction aimed at helping her become self-motivated and disciplined in her approach to learning
d. Strategies to help her understand the general meaning so that she can gather context clues

23. Of the following, which has been found to be the greatest challenge associated with professional development?

a. Finding time to schedule professional development and do follow-up
b. Developing seminars on the implementation of new educational standards
c. Addressing the changing forms of student assessment
d. Providing guidelines for working with diverse populations

24. Ms. Ross introduces new vocabulary words to her class daily. She then assigns reading that includes these words, uses these words in her speech as she presents lessons, and points them out when they appear in other contexts. Which instructional method does this represent?

a. Appropriate word choice
b. Teaching of word analysis
c. Using contextual analysis
d. Multiple word exposures

25. The Individuals with Disabilities Education Act (IDEA) requires that members of an IEP team include:

a. All teachers involved with the student, the parent(s) or guardian, and the student (if appropriate)
b. The classroom teacher, a special education teacher, the parent(s) or guardian, a representative of the local education agency knowledgeable about specialized instruction, someone to interpret instructional implications, the student (if appropriate), and other people invited by the parents or the school
c. The classroom teacher, a special education teacher, the principal or AP, and the parent(s) or guardian
d. All teachers involved with the student, the principal or AP, the parent(s) or guardian, and the student (if appropriate)

26. Which of the following does NOT describe a proper function of behavior rating scales?

a. To obtain judgments of a student's behavior in a standardized format
b. To screen students to obtain information about specific behaviors
c. To monitor the progress of students with severe behavior concerns
d. To classify students as having psychological problems

27. When selecting a functional curriculum for a high school class focusing on independent living skills, what would be the most essential to include in the curriculum?

a. Cooking
b. Laundry
c. Personal hygiene
d. Shopping

28. Mary is a 10-year-old student who has a developmental disability due to a physical impairment. Why would she NOT be eligible for special education services as a student with a developmental delay?

a. The developmental delay category does not include physical impairments.
b. The developmental delay category does not include students older than age 9.
c. The developmental delay category does not include students with developmental disabilities.
d. The developmental delay category does not include students younger than age 12.

29. What was the first major federal law guaranteeing all children aged 5–21 the right to a public education?

a. IDEA
b. EHA
c. FAPE
d. LRE

30. Phonemic drills are most appropriate for remediating which of the following?

a. Voice disorders
b. Fluency disorders
c. Language disorders
d. Articulation disorders

31. How would the use of a supplementary curriculum be most appropriate for a group of high school students in a social studies class?

a. Providing the students with accommodations to access the curriculum
b. Providing the students opportunities to explore careers
c. Providing the students use of assistive technology
d. Providing the students extra credit for additional assignments

32. Sandra is a special education teacher. At the facility where she works, which serves many students with multiple physical disabilities, the occupational therapist schedules regular OT clinics. Of the staff at this facility, who should attend these OT clinics?

a. The OT who plans the clinic, other OTs and OT aides, and the physical therapist
b. The OT staff, the direct care workers, the nurse, and the physical therapist
c. The OT staff, the doctor, and the nurses
d. The OT staff, PT staff, nurses, teachers, activity therapist, direct care workers, and behavior specialist

33. Howard Gardner's theory of multiple intelligences organizes learners into what types of intelligences?

a. Verbal-linguistic, mathematical, musically attuned, visual-spatial, body embraced, interpersonal, naturalistic, existential
b. Empathic, recessive, aggressive, assertive, dogmatic, apologetic, determined, elusive
c. Verbal-linguistic, logical-mathematical, musical, visual-spatial, bodily-kinesthetic, interpersonal, intrapersonal, naturalistic, existential
d. Dramatic, musical, verbal, mathematical, dance-oriented, sports-oriented, scientific, socially concerned

34. Jenny is a student teacher majoring in special education. She is working with a small group of students who are six years old and have mild developmental delays. She wants to give them some Piagetian tasks to try. Which of these would be most appropriate?

a. Tasks involving conservation of numbers, using rows of the same number of pennies, pebbles, or beads, arranged different distances apart
b. Class inclusion tasks using pictures and a 20-questions game to figure out which one the teacher is thinking of
c. Tasks involving conservation of weight, using boxes filled with sand arranged differently (e.g., stacked or side by side)
d. Tasks involving conservation of volume, using liquid in differently shaped containers (e.g., a tall, skinny container and a short, wide container)

35. Dustin is a ninth-grade student who struggles with his organizational skills. Which of the following assistive technology devices would be most beneficial in helping him improve these skills?

a. FM listening systems
b. Speech recognition programs
c. Data managers
d. Abbreviation expanders

36. Which instructional strategy would be most beneficial in working with a small group of seventh graders who struggle with math calculations?

a. Using worksheets
b. Using flash cards
c. Using visual aids
d. Using group projects

37. Which of the following statements regarding disability classification systems is most accurate?

a. There is a standardized, universal classification policy for disabilities in education.
b. There is little disparity among different disability classification systems in education.
c. Educators do not often experience difficulties in using the current classification procedures.
d. The identification of students for special education services is subject to much debate.

38. According to IDEA, when would it be appropriate for a due process to occur with regard to a student's IEP?

a. When the parents disagree with the decisions of the IEP team
b. When a student needs additional accommodations
c. When the parents request an evaluation
d. When a student no longer requires special education services

39. Which of the following is the best description of maintaining a previously learned skill?

a. Performing the skill in a variety of settings
b. Practicing the skill when it is learned
c. Progressing on the learned skill
d. Continuing to practice the learned skill

40. A student with ___________ has a great deal of difficulty with the mechanical act of writing. She drops her pencil, cannot form legible letters and cannot decode what she has written.

a. A nonverbal learning disorder
b. Dyslexia
c. Dyspraxia
d. Dysgraphia

41. A four-year-old child has difficulty sorting plastic cubes, circles, and triangles by shape, doesn't recognize patterns easily, and doesn't understand the relationship between little/big, tall/short, many/few. The child enjoys counting but does not say the numbers in proper order nor recognize the meaning of different numbers. This child most likely:

a. Has dyspraxia
b. Is developing within an acceptable range
c. Has dysgraphia
d. Has dyscalculia

42. Which of the following is true regarding teaching spelling?

a. Students who have an understanding of letter-sound association do not need to be taught to spell. If they can sound out a word, they can spell it.
b. Students who are able to determine the origin of a root word (Latin, Greek, Indo-European, etc.) can usually deduce the correct spelling of a word and do not require direct instruction in spelling.
c. Drilling spelling exercises is the most effective long-term method of teaching spelling.
d. By applying spelling patterns found in word families, the spelling of many words can be deduced.

43. When does current federal legislation (IDEA 2004) require transition planning for students with disabilities to begin?

a. At age 18
b. At age 22
c. At age 14
d. At age 16

44. Which of the following strategies is likely to be most effective in overcoming any kind of personal cultural biases when working with students with disabilities?

a. Learning about why the cultural bias occurs
b. Being objective when evaluating these students
c. Treating each of the students the same way
d. Encouraging cross-group participation among peers

45. Of the following instructional strategies used, which is most likely to support LD students in taking risks during reading lessons in a large group/class setting?

a. Assigning students to pairs to discuss teacher questions about the lesson
b. Asking students to give summaries reviewing the main points of a lesson
c. Having students complete reminder worksheets at the end of the lesson
d. Inviting students to ask "who," "what," or "where" questions on a lesson

46. When a student's behavior warrants alternative placement, how should the school determine appropriate placement?

a. Contact the student's parents and have them decide what is best for the student.
b. Talk to the student and let him or her choose the best placement.
c. Convene the placement review committee.
d. Suspend the student during an investigation.

47. Bert and Nan are first graders receiving special education. They each have an IEP objective in reading/phonological awareness to produce rhyming words and distinguish rhyming from non-rhyming words. Bert is blind, and Nan has cerebral palsy with poor fine motor skills. Which of the following would be the best plan for both students to work on this objective?

a. Give both a worksheet with a list of word pairs and have each student circle the pairs that rhyme and cross through the pairs that do not rhyme.
b. Read a list of word pairs to both students and have each raise the left hand if the words do not rhyme and the right hand if they do rhyme.
c. Give Nan a worksheet with a list of word pairs, having her circle the rhyming pairs and cross out the non-rhyming pairs; read word pairs to Bert and have him raise his right or left hand to indicate if they rhyme or not.
d. Give Nan a list of word pairs, have her read them to Bert, and have him indicate by which hand he raises whether they rhyme or not.

48. The left side of which lobe of the brain is most involved with mathematical calculations?

a. Parietal
b. Frontal
c. Occipital
d. Temporal

49. Which of the following disability categories would a student with a developmental disability most likely be eligible for under IDEA?

a. Emotional disturbance
b. Autism spectrum disorder
c. Speech or language impairment
d. Specific learning disability

50. The desired outcomes a teacher places on their students can also be referred to as what?

a. Goals
b. Expectations
c. Rules
d. Procedures

51. Which of the following best describes one of the roles of the special education paraprofessional in a middle school setting?

a. Toileting students with disabilities
b. Collaborating with general education teachers
c. Communicating with parents
d. Attending IEP meetings

52. When working with a group of eighth-grade students with writing deficiencies who struggle to stay on topic when writing, which of the following intervention strategies would be most appropriate?

a. Providing a graphic organizer for the students to use
b. Modeling the writing for the students
c. Providing opportunities for the students to practice
d. Allowing students to collaborate with peers

53. Which consequence would be the LEAST appropriate for a third-grade student with behavioral issues?

a. Having the student stay in during recess
b. Having the student go to a time-out area during class
c. Having the student fill out a points sheet when they display poor behavior
d. Having the student skip a fun activity at the end of the day

54. How can the interpretation of curriculum-based assessments be valuable in determining the growth of a student?

a. By comparing the student's score to others in the district
b. By comparing the student's score to their grade in the class
c. By comparing the student's score to the average score
d. By comparing the student's score to their previous scores

55. Which one of the following challenges is LEAST likely to arise when collaborating with parents at IEP meetings?

a. Differences with regard to IEP goals
b. Differences with regard to accommodations
c. Differences with regard to attendance issues
d. Differences with regard to service delivery

56. Stan needs to have a new IEP written this year. Of the following, who should attend the planning meeting?

a. Stan's teacher, his school psychologist, his speech therapist, and the school nurse should attend.
b. The teacher, school psychologist, all therapists, the nurse, Stan's parents, and Stan should attend.
c. Only Stan, his parents, his teachers, and the school psychologist need to attend.
d. Stan's parents, the teacher, and the school psychologist should be in attendance.

57. According to research findings, which of these is NOT a recommendation for improving the writing skills of students with learning disabilities?

a. Teaching students to set specific, attainable goals for writing
b. Teaching students strategies for planning, editing, and revising
c. Teaching students to avoid using writing for content learning
d. Teaching students how to use PC word processing programs

58. Mr. Hunt is a special education teacher with an elementary school class. He has one teacher's aide, one paraprofessional, and one parent volunteer, a mother, in his classroom. He uses peer tutoring methods as well. Three students—Marc, Fran, and Joe—have physical disabilities requiring assistance with snack time, bathroom breaks, and arts and crafts projects. One student, Clarence, likes to work alone on his math problems, but it is very important to him to have an adult check his work when he is done. Another student, Misty, is also very independent in her writing and art projects, but she needs the emotional support of periodic encouragement on her progress and praise for her results when she is done. Daisy and Carmela are similar in age and educational level and are friends, but Daisy excels in math and is below grade level in reading, while Carmela reads above her grade level but is below grade level in math. Which scenario is an example of the best use of Mr. Hunt's human resources in his classroom?

a. The paraprofessional assists Marc, Fran, and Joe with snacks, bathroom breaks, and arts and crafts projects; the teacher's aide checks Clarence's work and reports to Mr. Hunt so Mr. Hunt can explain Clarence's errors to him and assign additional exercises; the parent volunteer encourages and praises Misty; and Daisy and Carmela take turns helping each other in math and reading.
b. The paraprofessional checks Clarence's work, explains his errors, and assigns additional exercises; the parent volunteer takes Marc, Fran, and Joe to the bathroom; the teacher's aide helps with snacks; Daisy and Carmela take turns encouraging and praising Misty; and Mr. Hunt helps Marc, Fran, and Joe with arts and crafts projects.
c. Mr. Hunt takes Marc, Fran, and Joe to the bathroom; the parent volunteer checks Clarence's work, explains his errors, and assigns him additional exercises, and she helps with snacks; the paraprofessional helps Daisy with her reading and helps Marc, Fran, and Joe with arts and crafts; and the teacher's aide helps Carmela with her math.
d. Mr. Hunt encourages and praises Misty; Mr. Hunt helps Marc, Fran, and Joe with arts and crafts and takes them to the bathroom; the teacher's aide helps Marc, Fran, and Joe with snacks; the paraprofessional helps Carmela with math and Daisy with reading; and the parent volunteer checks Clarence's work, explains his errors, and assigns him additional exercises.

59. Ms. Harris has a special education classroom in a school with a multicultural population. This year her class includes Asian children, Native American children, and Hispanic children. The students have been placed in her class appropriately in terms of their types and severity of disabilities and educational levels. Knowing her students' cultural backgrounds, Ms. Harris has devised classroom strategies to facilitate their learning. Which of these is most likely one of her strategies?

a. Strictly enforcing individual work by each student and punishing cheating
b. Setting up collaborative learning group projects among all of the students
c. Assigning each student a turn at teaching the class to foster leadership
d. Setting up a high-stakes contest among the students and posting scores

60. Compared to a child with typical development, a child with spina bifida would be most likely to demonstrate deficits in:

a. Intellectual development
b. Language development
c. Motor development
d. Social development

61. Which of the following is true of the Family Educational Rights and Privacy Act with regard to students who receive special education services?

a. These protections also apply to private schools.
b. The school cannot release records without parental consent.
c. Parents do not have the right to request educational records.
d. Parental rights belong to the student when they turn 18.

62. Jared is a fifth-grade student with Down syndrome. Which of the following co-occurring conditions is Jared most likely to suffer from over the course of his life?

a. Heart disease
b. Traumatic brain injuries
c. Diabetes
d. Depression

63. Which one of the following education service providers gives instructional assistance to students who receive special education services?

a. Teaching assistants
b. Paraprofessionals
c. Student teachers
d. Behavior support professionals

64. Which of the following research-based intervention strategies would be most appropriate for a third-grade student who is working on basic decoding skills?

a. Multisensory techniques
b. Metacognitive strategies
c. Text structuring
d. Explicit teaching

65. Behavior problems in special education students are most effectively handled with:

a. Zero tolerance
b. Positive Behavioral Support (PBS)
c. Acceptance and tolerance
d. Positive Behavioral Control (PBC)

66. Which of the following is an example of an early intervention service for a student who is being evaluated for a developmental disability?

a. Speech services
b. Academic services
c. Counseling services
d. Adaptive services

67. Jimmy's behaviors disrupt his classroom daily. What is the first step the teacher and other school staff should take?

a. Refer Jimmy to receive special education services for a conduct or behavior disorder.
b. Conduct a functional behavior analysis to determine the purpose(s) of the behaviors.
c. Transfer Jimmy to a separate classroom reserved for students with behavior problems.
d. Recommend to parents that Jimmy be placed in a special school for problem students.

68. Which of the following is NOT true with regard to the role of parental participation in the IEP process?

a. Parents are members of the IEP team.
b. Parents can call an IEP meeting.
c. Parents can run an IEP meeting.
d. Parents can help develop IEP goals.

69. A new teacher is faced with a difficult student. The teacher has provided the appropriate warnings and stated classroom discipline methods. What is the next step for the teacher?

a. Continue to discipline the student.
b. Send the student in the hall.
c. Send the student to the principal.
d. Contact the student's parents.

70. Which of the following is correct about classroom modifications for students with disabilities?

a. Teachers rarely make incidental adaptations to address immediate problems.
b. Comprehensive plans for students with disabilities should include adaptations.
c. Classroom modifications made on the spot are unnecessary and inappropriate.
d. Teachers' intentional, planned adaptations are unlikely to meet student needs.

71. Ms. Banus is certified in speech-language pathology and audiology. Which professional organization membership does she hold to facilitate her services to students, their families, and her colleagues?

a. AAIDD
b. ASHA
c. APA
d. CCBD

72. Braden is a 10th-grade student with a specific learning disability. Which one of the following examples best describes when the results of his standardized testing may be invalid?

a. If Braden did not test at the appropriate instructional level
b. If Braden did not access his accommodations
c. If Braden did not take the alternate assessment
d. If Braden did not receive proper instruction

73. Justin is a ninth-grade student with a specific learning disability in the area of reading comprehension. Which of the following strategies would be most effective in ensuring that he maintains his knowledge of a story?

a. Asking him to read the story three times in a row
b. Asking him to reread the story for homework
c. Asking him to reread the story each week
d. Asking him to quiz himself on the story

74. A resource teacher wants to design a lesson that will help first and second graders learn irregular sight words so all the students can read their lists. She should teach them how to:

a. Divide sight words into syllables. Considering one syllable at a time provides a sense of control and increases confidence.
b. Recognize word families. Organizing similar words allows patterns to emerge.
c. Sound out the words by vocalizing each letter. Using this approach, students will be able to sound out any sight word.
d. Memorize their lists by using techniques such as songs, mnemonic devices, and other fun activities. By definition, irregular sight words cannot be decoded but must be recognized on sight.

75. By law, a child with a disability is defined as:

a. A child with intellectual disabilities; hearing, speech, language, visual, orthopedic, or other health impairments; emotional disturbance; autism; brain injury caused by trauma; or specific learning disabilities who needs special education and related services.
b. A child with intellectual disabilities, emotional disturbance, autism, brain injury caused by trauma, or specific learning disabilities who needs special education and related services.
c. A child who is unable to reach the same academic goals as his peers, regardless of cause, and needs special education and related services.
d. The term disability is no longer used. The correct term is other ability.

76. Which of the following is accurate regarding federal and state public health services?

a. The federal government funds and controls every state's delivery of public health services.
b. The federal government funds but delegates to the states to organize and deliver services.
c. In all states, public health agencies are freestanding agencies that function on their own.
d. In all states, public health is under the umbrella of the US Health & Human Services Department.

77. Which of the following professionals is least likely to work directly with high-needs students in the classroom?

a. Pediatrician
b. Occupational therapist
c. Speech-language pathologist
d. Counselor

78. Elise is a behavior specialist with a group of students who have various disabilities. One student has memory deficits. Another student has perceptual problems. A third student is diagnosed with difficulties in language processing. And a fourth student has IEP objectives to learn better problem-solving skills. In her research, which of the following would be a useful class of publications for Elise to read?

a. Journals of cognitive psychology
b. Journals of applied behavior analysis
c. Journals of the American Medical Association
d. Journals of neuroscience research

79. In core activities to teach phonological awareness, what would typically be introduced the earliest?

a. Phoneme blending
b. Phoneme segmenting
c. Initial phoneme identification
d. Phoneme substitution

80. Which of the following best describes the purpose of the prior written notice section of the IEP?

a. To invite parents to the IEP meeting
b. To provide copies of rights to parents
c. To propose changes to the IEP
d. To end special education services

81. What is an example of a modification of the curriculum?

a. Access to textbooks with larger print
b. Access to a computer to type assignments
c. Access to manipulatives
d. Access to alternative books

82. Which of the following would LEAST likely be one of the responsibilities of the school psychologist with regard to providing support for students with disabilities?

a. Providing mental health support
b. Administering IQ tests to students
c. Training staff on behavior plan implementation
d. Providing special education instruction

83. Which of the following is generally the strongest environmental factor influencing whether an individual with a disability is able to achieve positive life outcomes?

a. The type of disability that the person has
b. The personality of the individual with the disability
c. The meaning of the disability to the individual
d. The support system that the individual has

84. Which of the following best explains why learning objectives should be time-bound?

a. Objectives should explain the progress toward achievement.
b. Objectives should require a reasonable amount of resources.
c. Objectives should lead to a desired goal.
d. Objectives should include a date in relation to the accomplishment.

85. Albert Bandura's research found that observation of modeling:

a. Can never produce results like hands-on learning
b. Will work in real life but not from viewing video
c. Can have an impact equal to firsthand experience
d. Improves skill learning but doesn't affect behavior

86. Which of the following best describes how students who receive special education services are also protected under Section 504 of the Rehabilitation Act of 1973?

a. Students who receive special education services also receive 504 Plans.
b. Students who exit special education must receive 504 Plans.
c. Students with 504 Plans also receive special education services.
d. Students who received special education services prior to graduating high school can qualify for 504 Plans in college.

87. Ricky is a seventh-grade student being evaluated for special education services who is administered an IQ test. Which of the following best describes the results of his test if he scored a 100?

a. Ricky scored in the average range.
b. Ricky got all the questions correct.
c. Ricky does not need special education services.
d. Ricky does need special education services.

88. Sasha is a kindergarten student who seems to be struggling with the curriculum in her class. Which of the following screening tests would be LEAST likely to benefit Sasha before determining whether or not a special education evaluation is appropriate?

a. Communication screening
b. Hearing and vision screening
c. Motor skills screening
d. Cognitive screening

89. A high school student has been diagnosed with oppositional defiant disorder. Some of the manifestations of the diagnosis are:

a. He engages in obsessive and compulsive activities such as hand washing, counting, and ritualistic behaviors.
b. He is self-occupied, depressed, and disorganized. He keeps to himself, is considered odd by his classmates, and could be suicidal.
c. The student is overly occupied with others, defending them from imagined slights and determined they recognize his concern as real rather than psychotic.
d. He goes out of his way to annoy others, is defiant, and goes into childish rages in which he blames others.

90. Which of the following is LEAST likely to explain the gender gap in identification of boys and girls for learning disabilities?

a. Girls are less likely to show symptoms that prompt teacher referrals.
b. Boys are referred for evaluation more often due to a behavior bias.
c. Some assessment tools are more sensitive to learning profiles more typical of boys.
d. Expectations tend to be higher for girls.

91. Which of the following is the most correct statement about manipulatives for teaching math in grades K–12?

a. They are only efficacious when they are actual physical objects.
b. They help make an abstract subject more concrete for learners.
c. They are not yet available virtually on personal computers and so would not work.
d. They actively engage students less than traditional math classes.

92. Max is a fourth-grade student with a visual impairment. Which of the following would be most appropriate in supplementing his math curriculum?

a. Reading the problems to him orally
b. Allowing him extra time to work
c. Providing opportunities for hands-on experiences
d. Allowing him to use a computer

93. How might a lesson introduction be most beneficial when teaching students with learning disabilities about math?

a. To provide students with additional information
b. To ensure that students understand the curriculum
c. To connect the learning from the previous lesson
d. To challenge the students to learn as much as possible

94. Which of the following is a disadvantage of an externally facilitated IEP meeting?

a. The discussion can often get off topic.
b. It can be difficult to resolve conflicts.
c. It can make certain members feel left out.
d. It takes more time to prepare.

95. Jose is a fourth-grade student who was recently determined to be eligible for special education services. Which of the following strategies would be most beneficial in supporting his family?

a. Providing them with fact sheets about his disability
b. Holding informational meetings regularly
c. Allowing them to shadow his classes
d. Giving them a list of outside providers

96. Students with learning disabilities will typically spend part or all of their day in what type of classroom?

a. General classroom
b. Solitary classroom
c. Special education classroom
d. Language learning classroom

97. Alex is a ninth-grade student who receives services as a student with a traumatic brain injury. In order to be eligible to receive services under this disability category, which of the following causes of the injury can be ruled out?

a. Birth trauma
b. Combat injuries
c. Violence
d. Sports-related injuries

98. Fernando's family recently immigrated from a rural village in Mexico to a suburb in Texas. Upon admission to school, Fernando is given the same IQ and achievement tests that all elementary school children are given. His scores place him in the borderline intellectually disabled range and he is placed in a special education class with students who have developmental delays. Fernando's parents are puzzled at this since they always considered him normal at home, but being new to the United States and not speaking much English yet, they don't know what to do and think maybe this is just the way American schools do things. If you were a teacher in Fernando's new school, what would you recommend here?

a. Fernando's placement is appropriate because the tests are standardized objective measures and the numbers don't lie.
b. Fernando's borderline scores could be the result of coming from a rural community where he had no formal education rather than the result of a cognitive disability.
c. Fernando's scores reflect the fact that he and his parents speak Spanish at home and know very little English. He should be retested after sufficient ESL instruction.
d. Fernando's test scores were negatively affected by his culture shock at moving to a new country. He should be retested once he becomes acclimated to the United States.

99. Derrick is a student with profound intellectual disabilities and cerebral palsy. He can only use one arm and hand. He cannot speak but has good receptive language skills. His eyesight is good and he is cooperative. His teacher, Sam, needs to write some career skills in Derrick's IEP. Which of these would be a potential job for Derrick, for which Sam can write learning objectives?

a. Assembly of small machine parts
b. Sorting of small machine parts
c. Assembly line work with machine parts
d. Requisitioning and ordering machine parts

100. Which of the following is NOT one of the dispute-resolution processes that a parent or stakeholder may choose for a child with a disability who receives special education services?

a. Filing a complaint with the Department of Education
b. Asking to find a compromise through mediation
c. Filing a due process complaint
d. Removing the student from the school

Answer Key and Explanations for Test #1

1. A: The use of manipulatives in which students get to use their hands can help them learn new concepts, especially in math. Being able to see where objects go and touching the objects allow students with intellectual disabilities to get more involved. Although these students are often visual learners, manipulatives can help in areas such as math and science. Answer B is incorrect because enjoyment is not an instructional justification. Answer C is incorrect because manipulatives are not designed to help students learn classroom rules. Answer D is incorrect because manipulatives typically do not help students communicate.

2. C: In planning lessons, teachers need to consider the skill or concept they want to teach and be sure to define it and not assume they already know what it is (A). They need to identify the prerequisites that students need to learn the new material, not assume that they already have them (B). They need to consider what is required for the students to master the material being taught (C). They should also think about how they can expand what they have taught and how to show students to apply their new learning in useful ways. Such planning is not premature (D) and should be part of the lesson plans.

3. B: Taking academic classes would provide no job training and no transition to the workshop. Rebecca would need more training at the workshop to get up to speed. This is not the best plan. Therefore, option A is incorrect.

Rebecca can learn job skills first in the training center and then, when she is ready, she can be transitioned to the workshop, where she can actually do work and earn some money. Therefore, option B is correct.

If she were placed directly in the workshop, Rebecca would not be prepared since she has no job skills. She needs training first. Therefore, option C is incorrect.

A classroom at the training center is a good place for Rebecca to learn some job skills. However, staying there indefinitely would be like staying in school indefinitely. The workshop, though sheltered for disabled individuals, is still closer to a real workplace than a school, and she can earn money there. After going to school, she should make the transition to having a job. Therefore, option D is incorrect.

4. A: Mr. John's lesson plan is based around a boys' basketball team. Ms. Deere objects to this because their class is coeducational, and girls are less likely to relate to scenarios about an all-boy team. Girls can also play basketball. The female students will probably feel left out when considering this scenario. Therefore option A is correct.

There is no reason students with hearing impairments could not play basketball with some accommodations, so they could relate to this scenario. Even if none of them has ever played basketball, they have probably all seen a basketball game by the time they are in high school (on TV if not live). Therefore option B is incorrect.

It is possible that Ms. Deere could resent Mr. John having written the lesson plan without her input. But this is not the most valid reason for her objection. If it were, the question would not state specifically that Ms. Deere feels the lesson is biased. Therefore option C is incorrect.

While the lesson plan does involve a physical education/sport activity, this does not mean that no academics are involved. The question states that the plan is for multimodal activities. The students will thus be doing a variety of activities using different media and modes of learning and expression. So academic exercises such as writing essays and taking quizzes or tests could easily be parts of the lesson plan. Therefore option D is incorrect.

5. D: These are all examples of AT (d) that could be used in assessment. Not all AT need be "high-tech." A pencil wrapped with tape (a) could assist a student who has difficulty grasping writing implements in completing a written questionnaire. A text-to-speech-enabled computer (b) could assist students whose speech is impaired or absent, who have difficulty with verbal interactions, or have visual impairments, in responding to test questions or items. A computer's word processing program (c) can assist students with dysgraphia (writing disability), as well as problems with spelling, vocabulary, syntax, processing, and so on in responding to test items.

6. D: Students should always be warned that time-out is a potential consequence of their actions. The purpose behind this approach should always be to give the student time to think about his or her actions and to understand that certain behaviors are unacceptable in class. This consequence should never be used to shame or torture the child; therefore, it should always be connected to the undesired behavior before and after the event. By warning and then debriefing the child, he or she will have a better understanding of why the removal from the group was necessary. Forcing the child to apologize or to sit in repeated time-outs defeats the purpose of engaging the child in understanding and striving for better behavior.

7. A: A special education teacher should know how to serve as a resource person for families. By finding a group to fix Carly's chair at no charge, the teacher does this. Therefore, option A is correct.

Serving as a resource person for her student's family is part of the teacher's job. Therefore, option B is incorrect.

Paying for the repair herself is inappropriate. It is also unrealistic given a teacher's salary. It could make Carly's parents feel uncomfortable as well. And if there is a group that makes free repairs, it is an unnecessary expenditure. Therefore, option C is incorrect.

A charitable donation of a free chair sounds good, but the question states that Carly is not happy without her own chair. She is accustomed to it and is uncomfortable in the loaner chair. A donated chair is not the same as having the chair she is used to, and it might also be uncomfortable. It would be better to repair the chair that she likes. Therefore, option D is incorrect.

8. A: Email writing is the most universally applicable lifelong writing skill among the options because it is used consistently across academic, professional, and personal contexts. Students will likely need support in the word usage and specifics of what to write in an email to various people. While essay writing, letter writing, and resume writing are also valuable skills, they are more context-specific or used less frequently across settings, making email writing the best answer given the emphasis on universal applicability.

9. B: Telling Nina simply to avoid the public library does not help to fulfill the goal of inclusion. It puts additional limits on a student who already has a disability. Restricting her library activities to the school does not give Nina the least restrictive environment. Therefore option A is incorrect.

The special education teacher should know how to foster respectful, beneficial relationships with professionals in the community. By supervising Nina she can aid her in using the public library while keeping her from disturbing the quiet and annoying the librarian. Teaching her to control the volume of her voice when she is in the public library may enable Nina to visit the library by herself in the future without disturbing the peace. Acting as a facilitator can change the librarian's negative attitude toward Nina and establish more friendly relations. This will eliminate the librarian's discrimination against Nina and will promote a more positive relationship between a student with a disability and a community professional. Therefore option B is correct.

Complaining to the principal is not taking responsibility as a teacher for collaborating with members of the community. Though the librarian is discriminating, complaining to the principal is a negative action. The school principal could not do anything beneficial unless he supervised Nina's library visits, which is a better role for the teacher to take. If he simply insisted to the librarian that she allow Nina to visit, the librarian would be further antagonized. Therefore option C is incorrect.

Sending Nina to the school psychologist for consolation would not change the situation itself. Counseling would be more appropriate for a situation that cannot be changed (i.e., to accept the fact that she has a disability). Therefore option D is incorrect.

10. A: School psychologists are trained to administer IQ tests to students. Although it is possible for the special education teacher to assist in this process, IQ tests are typically administered by the psychologist. Answer B is incorrect because achievement tests are most often administered by the special education teacher. Answer C is incorrect because progress monitoring is completed by the special education case manager. Answer D is incorrect because transition planning inventories are also administered by the special education teacher.

11. C: Students in elementary school do not typically attend their IEP meetings. These students are often too young to attend and understand the discussion at the meeting, so they are most often not invited to the meeting. It is important to understand a student's maturity level before inviting him or her to an important meeting to discuss the IEP. Answer A is incorrect because the school psychologist can be an important member of the IEP team for students with emotional disturbances in writing behavior plans or monitoring goals. Answer B is incorrect because the director of special education is also often invited to these IEP meetings. Answer D is incorrect because most school districts require a building administrator to attend IEP meetings as well.

12. B: For learning objectives to be measurable, they must be written in a way that can be quantifiably described. Answer B isn't measurable because it is impossible to quantify 20% of the English language. Answers A, C, and D are incorrect because they are all measurable. There are 26 letters in the alphabet, so answer A can be quantified. Half of a reading packet and one chapter of a book are also measurable quantities.

13. A: Students from impoverished urban settings often have no experience with a cup and saucer as a set that go together; they may never have seen these two objects together in real life. It would be logical to them that a cup goes on the table. This example demonstrates the cultural bias of many standardized tests. Therefore, option A is correct.

Whereas some children may suffer from cognitive impairment if they have been malnourished, this is not true of all children from poor urban families. When a lack of familiarity with certain cultural customs influences their choice, as in this cup and saucer example, it would be erroneous to assume instead that their language development is delayed without other objective proof of this. Therefore, option B is incorrect.

While there is a correlation between poverty and lower educational levels, it is not true that all people of lower income lack critical thinking skills or do not teach these skills to their children.

There are many other factors contributing to a complex issue such as urban poverty. Therefore, option C is incorrect.

It is not true that children living in poverty never read books at home. There are many families who have little financially or materially, but who are literate and even love to read. (Consider the childhoods of famous people like Abraham Lincoln, Frederick Douglass, or Oprah Winfrey. They were all extremely poor growing up and all loved to read.) Therefore, option D is incorrect.

14. C: Students with independent living skills goals will likely need some support in reaching their goals and will need to take it step by step. Researching ingredients is a great first step in knowing what is needed to make the meals. It is important that students are supported in their independent living skills goals while also being given a level of independence. Answer A is incorrect because just working in the cafeteria and cleaning likely will not prepare the student to cook a meal. Answer B is incorrect because shadowing at a restaurant may be fun for the student, but hands-on experiences are likely to be more beneficial. Answer D is incorrect because if students are making lunch each day, they likely do not need this goal.

15. B: For a class such as math, which tends to be book heavy and involves a lot of the work using the textbook, the most beneficial strategy to use for this student would be an audio version of the textbook. This way, the student can listen to the problems instead of reading them. Answer A is incorrect because although a modified assignment length may be helpful, it may not be necessary if the student is completing the entire assignment. Answer C is incorrect because although preferential seating might be helpful, it likely will not have as much of an impact as having access to the audio book. Answer D is incorrect because although having extended time may also help, it may or may not be accessed based on the needs of the student.

16. A: Although all of these agencies may be beneficial for certain students based on their individual needs, school-to-work agencies would likely provide the most direct help for students with learning disabilities obtaining and maintaining jobs.

17. A: Visual imagery is visual but not graphic, consisting of mental images that proficient readers form as they read, which can be taught through guided visualization. Graphic organizers are visual *and* graphic, such as physical pictures (on paper, chalkboard, or computer screens) rather than mental images. Venn diagrams (B) help to visualize comparisons and contrasts by using overlapping ovals or circles and placing shared features in overlaps. Concept maps (C) use boxes, circles, or other shapes containing words for concepts with lines or arrows drawn between them to indicate relationships or connections. Flow charts (D) aid in guiding decision-making and correctly sequencing the steps of an activity as well as showing hierarchical and organizational structures. Boxes are arranged and connected showing chronological order or positions in a hierarchy, and branches based on yes/no questions show alternative next steps.

18. D: Although each student may react differently to this support, it is important to seek help when it is warranted. Students that have or are suspected of having mental illnesses should be kept under a watchful eye, and help should be sought as soon as possible. For these students, it may be necessary to seek support from the school counselors even if the student is unaware. Answer A is incorrect because at-risk students may not want their parents to know about their concerns, and this may trigger some strong emotions. Answer B is incorrect because asking too many questions might make these students feel uncomfortable. Answer C is incorrect because leaving them alone may not be productive if they are struggling and need some support.

19. B: Although schools will do everything they can to provide students with disabilities the best possible education, this is not stated in the law. Schools must provide an appropriate education to students with disabilities, but this does not require maximizing best possible outcomes. It is important to ensure that students are receiving FAPE and have access to general education and special education services. The other options are components of FAPE.

20. B: Although some students may thrive in a structured routine, it is important for the teacher to be open to change and be flexible. It is possible that lesson plans or teaching strategies don't go as planned, so it is important for the teacher to be able to change the routine when needed. An overly rigid or structured routine could force the teacher and class into an ineffective plan. Students with disabilities will especially need flexibility from the teacher on a daily basis. Answer A is incorrect because every student in the class can benefit from a multisensory approach. Answer C is incorrect because developing clear rules and expectations allows the students to understand what they can and cannot do in the class. Answer D is incorrect because station learning can allow students to work with peers and learn using a variety of techniques.

21. A: In order to attain a measurable goal, there must be concrete evidence that the goal is or is not being met. Without this evidence, it is difficult to determine how much progress is being made and how much is left to accomplish. Goals that are measurable are crucial to refining exactly what it is that the goal is trying to achieve. Answer B is incorrect because a cost analysis is a component of an attainable goal. Answer C is incorrect because a clarified description may be beneficial for whether or not a goal is measurable, but it is more closely related to the specificity of the goal. Answer D is incorrect because overarching objectives are components of relevant goals.

22. A: Well-organized coaching in decoding, sight words, vocabulary and comprehension several times a week would be the most beneficial to improve this student's reading comprehension. The more systematic the lessons are, the better the chance the intervention will succeed.

23. A: Although answers B, C, and D are all challenging tasks of professional development, studies show that the biggest challenge is finding the time in the crowded school calendar to present the information and do follow-up. Answer B is certainly a challenge in that the development of seminars to teach how to implement new educational standards is often complex and limited by time restraints, but this challenge is just part of the business of professional development. Answer C is a challenge because addressing any form of change requires developing adequate explanations and demonstrating how to implement the changes, often while meeting resistance from the constituent audience. Answer D is a challenge because it involves intensive research into the diverse populations and figuring out best practices.

24. D: Ms. Ross is presenting new words in multiple exposures to enhance vocabulary acquisition. Appropriate word choice (A) entails selecting words that are best suited to the particular instruction. Teaching word analysis (B) entails identifying word roots, prefixes, and suffixes, which greatly facilitates figuring out the meanings of new words. Contextual analysis (C) involves figuring out the meanings of new words by the context in which they occur.

25. B: The classroom teacher, a special education teacher, parents or guardian, a representative of the local education agency knowledgeable about specialized instruction, someone to interpret instructional implications, the student if appropriate, and other people invited by the parents or the school are required members of an IEP team according to IDEA. IDEA defines the IEP team as a group of people responsible for developing, reviewing and revising the Individualized Education Program for a disabled student.

26. D: Although behavior rating scales can be useful for many reasons, classifying students as having psychological problems is not one of them. Simply using one test to determine whether or not a student has these issues is typically not appropriate. It might be beneficial to use an assessment like a behavior rating scale as part of a body of evidence in making a determination about a student. Answer A is incorrect because these scales can compare a student with his or her peers in order to determine appropriate behaviors. Answer B is incorrect because these scales can also be used to screen students for potential problems. Answer C is incorrect because behavior rating scales can help in monitoring the progress of students with severe behavior concerns over time.

27. C: When selecting a curriculum for functional skills, it is important to focus on tasks that will occur the most often. Personal hygiene is a skill that people do every single day, and it is a crucial skill to work on. Answer A is incorrect because although cooking is important, personal hygiene is more useful and vital. Answer B is incorrect because laundry is something that should be learned after personal hygiene skills have been mastered. Answer D is incorrect because people must be able to care for themselves and their bodies before they can go out shopping in the community.

28. B: In order to be eligible for the developmental delay category, students must be age 9 or younger. There are many impairments that are included within the category, but students must be a certain age. According to IDEA, a student like Mary would likely be eligible in a different category because of her developmental disability. Answer A is incorrect because the developmental delay category does include students with physical impairments. Answer C is incorrect because students with developmental disabilities such as physical or emotional impairments would be eligible for the category if they meet the age requirements. Answer D is incorrect because students younger than age 10 are included in the category.

29. B: The Education for All Handicapped Children Act, or Education for the Handicapped Act (EHA), was passed in 1975 (Public Law #94-142) to guarantee everyone with disabilities aged 5–21 a free appropriate public education, or FAPE (C). It stated that all students with disabilities must be educated as much as possible in the least restrictive environment, or LRE (D). In 1990, this law was reauthorized and renamed the Individuals with Disabilities Education Act, or IDEA (A). It was later amended in successive reauthorizations in 1991, 1997, and 2004.

30. D: Articulation disorders involve distortion, omission, and/or substitution of speech sounds. Phonemic drills give students practice in producing sounds correctly. Voice disorders (A) are (outside of surgery) remediated by such therapeutic techniques as breathing support and audio feedback, among others, but not phonemic drills. Fluency disorders (B) such as stuttering are treated with a variety of techniques, including the Schwartz passive inhalation method, the Van Riper Program, Mark Power's method, Hollin's Precision Fluency Shaping, and many others, but phonemic drilling has no relation to fluency. Language disorders (C) involve difficulties with processing the language one hears, reads, speaks, and/or writes, and are remediated using many different strategies, although none of them include phonemic drilling.

31. B: Supplementary curriculum is typically designed to provide opportunities for students to explore experiences that they might be interested in after high school. This may look different for each student, but it can be beneficial in providing students opportunities that they may not otherwise have. A supplementary curriculum can be used for all students but is typically designed for students who may need additional support in accessing a job after high school. Answer A is incorrect because supplementary curriculum typically does not simply mean that the students can access their accommodations. Answer C is incorrect because although assistive technology can be involved in supplementary curriculum, it may not always be. Answer D is incorrect because a supplementary curriculum is not meant to create more work for the students.

32. D: Planning for assistive services is not limited to OT and PT. All personnel who deliver services to the student should attend since they will need to know how the devices operate, so option A is incorrect.

OT, PT, direct care, and nurses should be informed, but so should others; therefore, option B is incorrect.

More than OT and nurses should attend. While doctors can provide information about the student's physical condition, many M.D.s do not attend these meetings because of various other demands on their time for medical services; therefore, option C is incorrect.

The personnel listed in this option, including the behavior specialist and teachers, will work directly with the student. They should have the information provided in the clinic and also have input regarding the student's educational needs and how these will impact planning for assistive technology; therefore, option D is correct.

33. C: Gardner's multiple-intelligences framework includes verbal-linguistic, logical-mathematical, musical, visual-spatial, bodily-kinesthetic, interpersonal, intrapersonal, naturalistic, and existential intelligences. Teachers can use this framework to vary instruction and provide multiple ways for students, including students with learning disabilities, to engage with content.

34. A: According to Piaget, elementary-school-age children are in the stage of concrete operations. They can understand mental operations and their reversibility for the first time. Piaget said that children develop certain conservation skills earlier and others later. Conservation of number develops earliest, usually around ages five to seven years. The children in this question have mild developmental delays. So it can be expected that some of them may have developed this understanding and some have not. This would be a good task to offer them at their age. Therefore, option A is correct.

Class inclusion is typically acquired around the age of seven or eight. These children are only six and also have mild developmental delays, so they may be a year or two behind other children in cognitive development. In tests with the 20-questions game, children six to eight with normal cognitive development would simply guess (e.g., "Is it a banana?"), whereas children aged nine to eleven would think in terms of categories (e.g., "Is it something you eat?"), showing the ability of classification. A class inclusion task for six-year-olds with mild developmental delays would be too advanced, and they would probably all fail at it. Therefore, option B is incorrect.

Conservation of weight usually develops around the ages of nine to ten. This would be beyond the development of cognitively average six-year-olds, let alone those with mild developmental delays. Therefore, option C is incorrect.

Conservation of volume is typically attained around the ages of twelve to fourteen, according to Piaget. It would be far beyond the cognitive abilities of six-year-olds. Therefore, option D is incorrect.

35. C: Although all these choices may be beneficial to students who struggle with organizational skills, data managers are the most effective in helping students organize tasks. These data managers allow students to put information on tasks into a system, and the system is instrumental in organizing it for them. Students with executive functioning skills can benefit from these tools in that they have to do less of the organization and management of information. Answer A is incorrect because FM listening devices are typically for students who struggle with hearing. Answer B is incorrect because speech recognition programs are designed for students who struggle with writing texts. Answer D is incorrect because abbreviation expanders are beneficial in helping students who may struggle with word processing.

36. C: Students who struggle with math calculations will likely need an alternative teaching method in order to memorize facts. These students have likely used many of the traditional methods but continue to struggle. The use of visual aids allows students to see the numbers in a different way, which allows them to find a new approach to memorizing these facts. Answer A is incorrect because worksheets do not provide these students with an opportunity to practice an alternative teaching method that they have not already seen. Answer B is incorrect because flash cards tend to be difficult for students who struggle with math because they are unable to memorize facts easily. Answer D is incorrect because although group projects may be beneficial to some students, their use may not support students who struggle with memorizing facts.

37. D: There is currently no universal, standardized policy for the classification of disabilities in education. Developing such a universal policy is a goal, or a dream, of many educators, but such a policy does not yet exist.

There is a good deal of disparity among different classification systems. This is one of the problems educators face in making disability classifications.

Educators face many dilemmas when using current disability classification procedures. This is due to many factors, such as disparity among different classification systems and the lack of a universal policy; the possibility that students are not classified accurately; the possibility that current systems may not produce adequate educational services; and the possibility that systems designed to promote equity may backfire and promote discrimination instead, just to name a few.

The identification and classification of students with disabilities for special education services is an issue of much controversy. The inherent difficulties of the classification procedure described here contribute to the long debate over this subject.

38. A: A due process can occur when the parents of a student receiving special education services disagree with a portion of or the entire IEP. The parents have a right to challenge the decisions that have been made, and a hearing is held to determine the next actions. It is important for parents to understand that they have these rights if they disagree with the decisions of the IEP team or school district. Answer B is incorrect because if the student needs additional accommodations, the team can amend the IEP. Answer C is incorrect because when the parents request an evaluation, the school must conduct a special education evaluation. Answer D is incorrect because if the student no longer requires services, that student will no longer have an IEP.

39. D: Maintenance is important in ensuring that students are able to retain the information that they have learned on a particular topic. In order to do this, the students must practice the skill regularly to ensure that it is not forgotten. Depending on the skill, this may mean daily, weekly, or monthly practice in order to maintain what has already been learned. Answer A is incorrect because performing the skill in a variety of settings would be an example of generalization. Answer B is incorrect because simply practicing the skill when it is learned may make it difficult to maintain the skill. Answer C is incorrect because progressing on the skill can be helpful, but this may not necessarily help in maintaining the learned skill.

40. D: Dysgraphia. Dysgraphic individuals cannot manage the physical act of writing. While many dysgraphics are highly intelligent and able to express themselves cogently, they have extreme difficulty holding a writing implement and shaping letters.

41. D: The child most likely has dyscalculia. Dyscalculia defines a range of difficulties in math, such as the inability to understand numbers' meanings, measurements, patterns, mathematical terms, and the application of mathematic principles. Early clues include a young child's inability to group items by size or color, recognize patterns, or understand the meaning or order of numbers.

42. D: Students should be taught that writing is a process. By applying spelling patterns found in word families, the spelling of many words can be deduced. The other options are incorrect statements regarding teaching spelling. It is not true that knowing letter-sound association is enough alone to know how to spell. Simply knowing the origin of the root word, though potentially helpful, does not make instruction unnecessary. Drilling spelling exercises is often not the most effective long-term method of teaching spelling, as it can lead to frustration and a lack of interest on the part of the students.

43. D: The 1997 version of IDEA required transition planning to begin when the student was 14 years old (C). The 2004 reauthorization of this law changed the age to 16. Some students with disabilities, such as those with autism spectrum disorders, often need extended time periods for transition planning, so many special educators still advocate beginning at age 14. Some individual states also specify age 14. The later age in the current reauthorization may reflect considerations related to developmental levels. Some students with disabilities need more time to complete secondary education. However, others will graduate at age 18 (A), so this can be too late for transition planning. (Under IDEA, legal rights to transition planning and services generally transfer from parents to students when students reach the age of majority as defined by state law, which is often 18.) Students with disabilities have the legal right to attend school until they graduate or reach the age of 22 (B), so transition planning must start before this.

44. A: Although all these strategies can be beneficial in overcoming cultural biases, learning why the bias occurs is likely to be the most effective. If teachers are able to analyze and understand why some of the biases occur, they may be able to eliminate them or overcome them. Cultural biases occur for many reasons, but it is important to understand the impact that a teacher has and what the needs of the student might be. Answer B is incorrect because being objective may not be quite as effective as showing empathy for certain students. Answer C is incorrect because not all students will likely learn the same way, so they should not necessarily be treated the same. Answer D is incorrect because simply encouraging these cross-group interactions may or may not help in overcoming personal biases.

45. D: Students with learning disabilities often avoid asking questions in large classes/groups. Teachers can encourage them to take risks by giving cues that support their asking "wh-" questions. Pairing students to discuss teacher questions (A) is a good strategy to engage all LD students in a large class. Asking LD students to summarize main lesson points (B) is a good strategy to discern whether they understand these, and reviewing benefits all students. Having LD students complete reminder worksheets at the end of the lesson (C) is a good strategy to see what they have learned, what they enjoyed, and what else they know about the subject.

46. C: A placement review committee consists of at least three members, two of whom are teachers. A teacher can refuse to participate on the committee. The committee conducts a thorough review of the student's behavior and makes a professional decision that considers both the needs of the student and the school. This committee must also take into consideration any disability the student might have, whether or not it is documented, and comply with the Americans with Disabilities Act, IDEA, and Section 504. While contacting the parents and speaking with the student are also good steps to take, a placement decision is decided by the placement review committee.

47. B: Since he is blind, Bert could not read a printed or written worksheet or circle and cross out word pairs. Therefore, option A is incorrect.

Both students could listen to word pairs read aloud. Even with poor fine motor skills, Nan has the gross motor skills to raise her hands. Therefore, option B is correct.

As Nan has poor fine motor skills, she might have difficulty circling or crossing out words, especially since she is only in first grade. Therefore, option C is incorrect.

Having Nan read a list of word pairs aloud to Bert would give Bert but not Nan the opportunity to show recognition of rhymes. Therefore, option D is incorrect.

48. A: Neuroimaging studies find that the left side of the (A) parietal lobe, located behind the frontal lobe at the back of the top of the brain, is most involved with mathematical calculations. The frontal (B) lobe is involved with speech, emotions, and executive functions such as solving problems, making decisions, and planning. The occipital (C) lobe is at the back of the brain and is responsible for the processing of information received through the sense of vision. The temporal (D) lobe is below the frontal and parietal lobes and is involved with aspects of speech, memory, perceiving and identifying auditory stimuli (sounds), and other functions. Damage in the parietal-temporal area can cause deficits in digit span and verbal memory.

49. B: According to IDEA, students who are determined eligible for services under the autism spectrum disorder category have a developmental disability. Students with developmental disabilities are impacted mentally or physically in many ways and tend to have severe long-term problems. Students with autism are typically impacted by struggling with verbal and nonverbal communication, which impacts their access to education. Answer A is incorrect because although students with emotional disturbances can also have a developmental disability, this would likely place them in the multiple disabilities category. Answer C is incorrect because students with only speech or language impairments have their own disability category. Answer D is incorrect because students with specific learning disabilities are typically impacted by their academic abilities.

50. B: A teacher's expectations are the desired result of their goals. On the other hand, goals are the means to obtaining the outcomes. For example, a goal may be to complete lesson one by the end of week one. This goal will determine the activities the teacher plans for that week. The teacher will also have the expectation that her student will complete and understand the lesson. Rules and procedures typically refer to acceptable behavior in the classroom. Effective classroom management will detail the rules of the classroom as well as the process to follow those rules. Taken together, well-thought-out goals, expectations, rules, and procedures will yield a well-run classroom.

51. A: One of the responsibilities of paraprofessionals in many schools is to toilet students with disabilities. This will typically involve students with severe needs who are unable to toilet themselves and need additional support in this area. Although this may not always be a requirement for every paraprofessional, it is often expected as a part of the fulfillment of the duties of the job. Answer B is incorrect because it is the responsibility of the special education teacher to collaborate with the general education teachers. Answer C is incorrect because communicating with parents should also be done by the special education teacher. Answer D is incorrect because paraprofessionals are not typically involved in IEP meetings.

52. A: Although all of these choices may be beneficial to certain students, providing a graphic organizer would be most beneficial for students who struggle with organizing their writing because it gives them a framework for how to set it up. Many students struggle to organize their writing and stay on topic, and the graphic organizer is designed to help with this. Answer B is incorrect because simply modeling the writing likely is not enough support for many students. Answer C is incorrect because practice without organizational support does not address the underlying difficulty. Answer D is incorrect because peer collaboration may support idea development, but it does not directly teach students how to structure and focus their writing.

53. A: Although each of these choices could be beneficial consequences for a third-grade student, having them skip recess is usually the least appropriate. Students with behavior needs often need sensory stimulation, which recess provides. It is also likely this student's favorite part of the day, and behavior may escalate if they have to skip it. Answer B could be an effective strategy in changing their behavior quickly. Answer C is beneficial in that a point sheet keeps them aware of and responsible for their own behavior. Answer D has the benefit of using behavioristic negative punishment that can help condition a reduction in negative behaviors, but it can be hard to make effective with students at this age as it is far removed from the action itself. For instance, if the student acts up at 9am, but the punishment does not take place until 2pm, the response may not be as strong as intended.

54. D: Curriculum-based assessments can be beneficial in determining how much progress a student is making on their goals. It is important to monitor the progress a student is making by giving them curriculum-based assessments that are directed toward their IEP goals. These data can help to guide instruction and determine if any changes need to be made so that the student makes continued progress toward that goal. Answer A is incorrect because comparing a student's score to others in the district would be a norm-referenced or standardized assessment. Answer B is incorrect because comparing a student's score to their grade in the class would likely be a summative assessment. Answer C is incorrect because comparing a student's score to the average score would likely be a norm-referenced assessment.

55. C: Although parents may discuss some of the issues they have with their child's attendance at the IEP meeting, this is not typically discussed at the meeting. Differences that arise from the IEP meeting will typically stem from the IEP itself. Because there is no section in the IEP that specifically discusses attendance issues, this is the least likely issue to arise. Answer A is incorrect because it is common for the parents and teacher to have differences with regard to the student's IEP goals. Answer B is incorrect because parents may disagree about some of the accommodations that their child has access to. Answer D is incorrect because some parents may also have differences of opinion regarding the service delivery section of the IEP.

56. B: The first option omits the student himself, Stan, as well as his parents. All involved school, home, and community parties should collaborate in IEP planning. Therefore, option A is incorrect.

Of the choices given, the second option includes the parties who should definitely be involved. There may be additional parties involved depending on the individual, but this option is the only one to include the student, his parents, his teachers, and other school personnel. It is the only one of the four choices that is not incomplete as to required attendees. Therefore, option B is correct.

Stan and his parents should attend, as should the teacher and school psychologist. But this choice states that these are the only parties who should attend. This is not true. Other people may be involved in Stan's education. Therefore, option C is incorrect.

The fourth option omits Stan. Therefore, option D is incorrect.

57. C: Research has found that using writing as a tool for learning academic content is helpful to normally achieving students and students with learning disabilities (LD), so teaching students to avoid this (C) is not a recommendation. Based on their findings, researchers recommend teaching students to set specific, attainable goals for what they will write (A). They advise teachers to instruct students in strategies for planning what they will write, editing what they have written, and making indicated revisions (B). Researchers also recommend that teachers give LD students instruction in using PC word processing programs (D), which can make many aspects of writing much easier for them.

58. A: The paraprofessional can assist with physical needs. The aide can check Clarence's work but should refer re-teaching and assignment of exercises to Mr. Hunt. The parent volunteer is a good choice to give Misty emotional support. Daisy and Carmela are the best choices for peer tutoring since they are very alike in age and grade level but are opposites when it comes to strengths and weaknesses in math and reading. Therefore, option A is correct.

The paraprofessional can check Clarence's work but should not explain or assign exercises. The teacher should do these things. The parent volunteer may or may not be comfortable taking children other than her own to the bathroom. Misty may appreciate the peer approval implicit in receiving emotional support from Daisy and Carmela, but she may also prefer adult approval. Since Daisy and Carmela's strengths and weaknesses are so opposite and their other characteristics are so similar, their helping each other is a more directly beneficial use of peer tutoring. If both girls are busy supporting Misty, they will have less time and attention to help each other and make their own progress. Although the teacher can give physical help with arts and crafts when he is the only adult in the class, since others are present who can help with this, he can do more teaching. Therefore, option B is incorrect.

As the teacher, Mr. Hunt should not be taking students to the bathroom while the volunteer, the paraprofessional, and the aide do his teaching tasks. Therefore, option C is incorrect.

In option D, Mr. Hunt is doing too many things considering how many helpers he has in his room. He is supporting Misty, helping the physically disabled students with arts and crafts, and also taking them to the bathroom. At the same time, the paraprofessional and the volunteer are doing his teaching tasks. Therefore, option D is incorrect.

59. B: Some of the children in Ms. Harris' class likely come from collectivist cultures. In America, individualism and competition are highly valued. In collectivist cultures, the good of the group and cooperation are more highly valued. Making these students work individually and not allowing them to work together or help each other would be at odds with their cultural backgrounds and values and would not be successful. Therefore, option A is incorrect.

Setting up collaborative learning groups who work together to complete a project would be congruent with these children's cultural mores and thus more likely to succeed. Therefore, option B is correct.

Allowing each student to teach class can be a valuable confidence booster in some circumstances. But in this case, many of the students would likely feel uncomfortable being in the spotlight as a result of being assigned a leadership role. These students' backgrounds tend to emphasize the importance of group identity over individual identity. Their cultures frown on the personal fame that is prized in American culture. Contributing to the collective public wellbeing is considered more honorable than individual identity in many cases. Therefore, option C is incorrect.

Some of the students in the classroom likely come from cultures that value cooperation above competition. In America, it is common for students to be encouraged, or even pushed, to strive for personal excellence and to be better than others. It is also common in American culture to publicize one's competitive success. Ms. Harris' students are likely to not agree with these practices. In their cultures, it is more common to sacrifice personal identity for the sake of the nation, the institution, or the family—i.e., the group. These students are more likely to feel pride in contributing to the whole than in standing out from the crowd. Therefore, option D is incorrect.

60. C: The effects of spina bifida vary in severity with the type of spina bifida and the individual who has it. The most likely effect is on motor development because the spinal column does not fuse completely, leaving an opening. Many children with spina bifida cannot walk, and the strength and mobility of the upper limbs and body can also be affected. Intellectual development (A) can be affected if cerebrospinal fluid backs up into the brain and the fluid buildup, called hydrocephalus, is not relieved by shunting; spina bifida without hydrocephalus does not cause brain damage. As long as intellectual development is not affected, language development (B) is not affected by spina bifida. This condition does not affect social development (D) as, for example, autism often does.

61. D: Parents have the right to access educational records, including IEPs, for students until they turn 18. Once a student turns 18, the parents no longer have the same rights and must request the records through the student. This is important when working with students with IEPs who go to college or transfer to a different school. Answer A is incorrect because these protections do not apply to private schools that do not receive public funding. Answer B is incorrect because there are cases in which the school can release these records without parental consent. Answer C is incorrect because parents do have the right to request educational records within a certain time period.

62. A: More than half of individuals born with Down syndrome also suffer from heart conditions throughout their lifetime. Although many of these develop when they are born, heart conditions can arise at any time. This can lead to high blood pressure and an inability to get blood pumped to the heart. Answer B is incorrect because although traumatic brain injuries can happen in individuals with Down syndrome, they are most often caused by external factors and can happen to anyone. Answer C is incorrect because although diabetes is often diagnosed in those with Down syndrome, heart diseases are the most common. Answer D is incorrect because depression is not as common as heart disease in those with Down syndrome.

63. B: Paraprofessionals provide instructional support to students with disabilities to ensure they have access to the curriculum. Paraprofessionals typically work under the guidance of special education teachers to make sure that students have the accommodations and modifications that they need. These professionals are instrumental in assisting the special education teacher and the general education teacher. Answer A is incorrect because teaching assistants can include a wide variety of people including student assistants or aides for general education classes. Answer C is incorrect because student teachers are typically students who are receiving on-the-job training to become teachers. Answer D is incorrect because behavior support professionals typically work on behavior deficits and not issues dealing with instructional assistance.

64. A: For a third-grade student working on basic decoding, multisensory techniques engage visual, auditory, and kinesthetic pathways to support accurate letter-sound decoding, helping students recognize and blend sounds into words. While explicit teaching, metacognitive strategies, and text structuring are valuable for reading comprehension and general instruction, they are less targeted to decoding skills. This realignment ensures the construct being tested (decoding) matches the correct answer.

65. B: Positive Behavioral Support is the most widely recommended and effective approach. The Individuals with Disabilities Education Act of 1997 requires schools to consider positive behavioral interventions and supports.

66. A: Early intervention services are designed to help young children who are struggling with basic skills. Speech or communication issues are common in younger children who struggle with talking or understanding. Early intervention services are important to identify the areas that need to be targeted right away in children. Answer B is incorrect because academic services would typically come after the student has worked on early intervention skills. Answer C is incorrect because counseling services wouldn't likely begin until students were older. Answer D is incorrect because adaptive services would likely apply to older students who struggle with everyday functions.

67. B: The first step is to determine what function(s) or purpose(s) the behaviors serve by conducting a functional behavior analysis (FBA). Students are not usually referred for special education without first trying classroom interventions determined through an FBA; also, a conduct or behavior disorder should not be assumed if it has not been diagnosed after thorough evaluation (A). Moving the student to a separate classroom (C) is also inappropriate. Even after the FBA, classroom interventions, referral if indicated, evaluation, diagnosis, and placement in special education if indicated, the least restrictive environment as dictated by law is more likely to be inclusive than segregated. Recommending special school placement to parents (D) is also premature and inappropriate.

68. C: Although parents have many rights with regard to their child's IEP, running the IEP is not one of those rights. Typically, the IEP meeting will be run by a special education teacher or administrator. Parents are encouraged to be highly involved in the IEP meeting, but they are not responsible for facilitating the meeting. Answer A is incorrect because parents are important members of the IEP team. Answer B is incorrect because parents can call an IEP meeting if they believe their child's needs must be addressed. Answer D is incorrect because parents can help to develop IEP goals.

69. C: Each teacher should have a list of school and classroom rules posted in their classroom. Also, students should be fully aware of the consequences of not following the rules. If a student is unruly, the teacher should act according to their stated rules and consequences, and if the student's behavior does not improve, sending that student to the principal's office is the next step. A teacher must keep in mind that while they need to enforce the rules, they are responsible for the safety and educational needs of the other students, as well.

70. B: It is important for teachers to include needed classroom adaptations in their comprehensive plans for students with disabilities. Many of the classroom changes that teachers make are incidental but provide an immediate solution when they notice some students having difficulties; this is not rare (A). These kinds of changes are usually both necessary and appropriate, not the reverse (C). Therefore, they are likely to meet those students' needs, not unlikely (D). However, incidental modifications alone are insufficient. As teachers come to know individual students, they should plan adaptations for the needs they can predict before starting a lesson.

71. B: AAIDD is the American Association on Intellectual and Developmental Disabilities. Typically a speech-language pathologist and audiologist will work with students who do not have intellectual disabilities as well as with those who do. She might have an AAIDD membership as well, but this would not be the primary choice of those listed. Therefore option A is incorrect.

ASHA is the American Speech and Hearing Association. This is the most logical primary choice for Ms. Banus. Therefore option B is correct.

APA is the American Psychological Association. Ms. Banus is not a psychologist or behavior specialist. Thus she is unlikely to be a member of this organization. Therefore option C is incorrect.

CCBD is the Council for Children with Behavioral Disorders. Ms. Banus has an equal probability of working with some students who also have behavior disorders and with many other students who do not. She does not specialize in behavioral disorders. Therefore option D is incorrect.

72. B: Although all of these factors may be taken into consideration, it is important for students to access their accommodations in order for the test to be valid. If a student like Braden did not have the accommodations that he is entitled to receive because of the impact of his disability, the test will not be valid. Many students with learning disabilities will have accommodations on standardized assessments such as extended time or oral presentation of the test. Answer a is incorrect because standardized tests do not necessarily align with what the students are learning in the classroom. Answer c is incorrect because the alternate assessment is designed for students who cannot access the typical standardized assessment. Answer d is incorrect because it may be difficult to determine what proper instruction looks like for specific students.

73. C: When maintaining a skill, it is important to practice that skill periodically over the course of time. For someone that struggles with reading comprehension, it is important to practice reading multiple times to ensure that the content is remembered. Students with disabilities who struggle in certain areas will likely need extra practice for maintaining these skills. Answer A is incorrect because simply reading the story a few times in a row will not allow the student to maintain the skill long-term. Answer B is incorrect because just rereading the story once for homework likely will not allow him to maintain the skill either. Answer D is incorrect because although quizzing himself may be a valuable strategy in helping him remember the story, it likely will not allow him to maintain this skill.

74. D: Memorize their lists by using techniques such as songs, mnemonic devices, and other fun activities. By definition, irregular sight words cannot be decoded but must be recognized on sight.

75. A: A child with intellectual disabilities; hearing, speech, language, visual, orthopedic, or other health impairments; emotional disturbance; autism; brain injury caused by trauma; or specific learning disabilities who needs special education and related services. Children with one or more of these conditions are legally entitled to services and programs designed to help them achieve at the highest level of their ability.

76. B: The federal government funds and supports public health systems, but it does not control the states' organization and delivery of public health services. Therefore, option A is incorrect. The federal government gives funding and support, but it delegates authority to each state to organize and deliver public health services, as dictated by the Constitution. Therefore, option B is correct. All states do not have freestanding public health agencies operating on their own. Some states have such agencies and some do not. Therefore, option C is incorrect. All states do not have umbrella organizations known as departments of health and human services. Some states do and some do not. Therefore, option D is incorrect.

77. A: Countless kinds of professionals are available to work with students in the classroom, including occupational therapists, speech and language pathologists, counselors, paraprofessionals, and specialized therapists for specific disorders. Procedures for classroom interventions will vary by school and system; however, most classrooms now hold some children who are differently-abled or who have special needs. This change means that outside professionals will often work with students in class. However, pediatricians are not typically found in classrooms. These doctors are usually involved in the educational process for specific patients, but they are not the experts most qualified to work with students on a day to day basis in the classroom.

78. A: Journals of cognitive psychology are concerned with research in the study of memory, language processing, perception, problem-solving, and thinking. These are the exact areas in which Elise's students have educational needs. Therefore, option A is correct.

Applied behavioral analysis means applying experimentally-derived principles of behavior with the goal of improving social behavior. Journals on this subject would not address the cognitive needs of Elise's students. Therefore, option B is incorrect.

The Journal of the American Medical Association (JAMA) is a professional medical journal publishing peer-reviewed original medical research. It is a very popular journal among doctors. Its research articles would not typically address cognitive concerns. Therefore, option C is incorrect.

Journals of neuroscience research publish research results about the development, functions, and diseases of the nervous system, using molecular, cellular, and systems approaches. Diseases of the nervous system can affect cognitive processes. However, this research is not as directly related to studying the particular cognitive deficits of Elise's students as the journals of cognitive psychology are. Therefore, option D is incorrect.

79. C: Initial phoneme identification is generally the first skill that is introduced. This involves identifying the sound at the beginning of a word. Phoneme blending is taking individual phonemes and combining them into a word, like blending /s/, /u/, and /n/ to make "sun." Phoneme segmenting (B) is the reverse of blending, or being able to identify the individual phonemes in a given word. In this case, given the word "sun," the student can break it down into /s/, /u/, and /n/. Students are also taught segmentation of initial, middle, and final phonemes. Phoneme substitution (D) involves the student's substituting one phoneme of a word to make another word. For example, with initial phonemes, given "cat," the student can make "sat," "mat," "hat," "bat," etc.

80. C: The prior written notice section of the IEP proposes changes that the team determines are necessary to provide free appropriate public education for the child with a disability. The prior written notice is often the last section of the IEP, and it describes the reason for the IEP meeting and the changes that were made. Although prior written notice must be provided prior to any change in special education services, it is also included as a section in the IEP. Answer A is incorrect because a notice of meeting would be an invitation to the parents for the IEP meeting. Answer B is incorrect because providing copies of parent rights typically has a separate section in the IEP. Answer D is incorrect because a separate form must be filled out to end special education services.

81. D: Modifications of the curriculum alter the curriculum that is being taught, and these students are expected to complete assessments different than those of their peers. Access to alternative books changes what the student is learning and therefore would change the expectations for the assignment. Answers A, B, and C are all accommodations that allow students to access the same curriculum as their peers with alterations to how the material is presented. Textbooks with large print, computers for typing, and manipulatives are all accommodations to allow students to access the curriculum.

82. D: The school psychologist does not typically provide special education instruction. Answer A is incorrect because school psychologists will often provide mental health support to students.

Answer B is incorrect because school psychologists are also often responsible for administering different kinds of tests, including IQ assessments. Answer C is incorrect because school psychologists can also assist special education teachers in training staff on implementing behavior support.

83. D: Although all of these factors can have an enormous impact on a person and everyone may be impacted in a different way, the support system is typically the most beneficial. Without a support system in place, which may include parents, siblings, or other friends or family members, it will be difficult for individuals with disabilities to follow their own path to making a positive impact on society. Research shows that individuals with disabilities are more likely to succeed when they have a positive support system. Answer A is incorrect because although the type of disability is certainly impactful, individuals with all kinds of disabilities can succeed with proper support. Answer B is incorrect because the personality is important, but it does not have as much of an impact as a support system in place. Answer C is incorrect because the meaning of the disability may or may not be impactful for some individuals.

84. D: In order for objectives to be time-bound, there must be a date that the objective is to be reached. This is important for ensuring that students are making adequate progress in a timely manner. If the objectives are not bound by time, then it is harder to evaluate progress and determine whether they have been achieved within an appropriate time frame. Answer A is incorrect because the progress toward the achievement is considered the measure of the goal. Answer B is incorrect because using a reasonable amount of resources shows how achievable an objective may be. Answer C is incorrect because the use of objectives leading to a desired goal is a component of relevant or realistic objectives.

85. C: Bandura's social learning theory incorporates observational learning, vicarious learning, and imitation of modeling. He found through his research that a child could observe another child receiving a reward or punishment and learn the same things through observation that the other child learned through direct experience. The belief that hands-on learning (A) was superior to observation was supported by Jean Piaget, not Bandura. Rather famously, Bandura also discovered that children who viewed violent videos did display more aggressive behavior as a result; observation of real-life aggression was not required (B). Bandura's pioneering work made parents and educators more aware of the impacts that media can have on children's behavior (D).

86. D: Students who receive special education services at the high school level no longer access these services when they graduate, but they can access 504 Plans. These plans are designed to provide accommodations to students with disabilities in college or beyond in the workplace. Although students with disabilities cannot continue to receive these special education services when they graduate high school, it is important for them to understand the types of support that are available to them. Answer A is incorrect because students who receive special education services most often do not also have a 504 Plan. Answer B is incorrect because students who exit from special education may or may not access a 504 Plan, but this is not required. Answer C is incorrect because students with 504 Plans are not entitled to special education services.

87. A: A score of 100 on a standard IQ test indicates a score that is right in the middle of the average range when compared to other students his age. This indicates that Ricky's intelligence is where it is expected to be for someone his age. Additional assessments are necessary to determine whether he does or does not need special education services, however. Answer B is incorrect because a score of 100 is in the middle of the data, not an indication that he scored 100% on the test. Answer C is incorrect because additional assessments must be conducted to determine his need for services. Answer D is incorrect because Ricky may not need services, depending on the results of other assessments.

88. D: Although it can certainly be beneficial to perform a cognitive screening on students, these typically come a little later than kindergarten. Many students in kindergarten are still developing, so a cognitive screening does not always provide the best results. These screening assessments are designed to determine what areas students are struggling with, but they can only be useful for age-appropriate activities. Answer A is incorrect because communication screenings can be valuable in determining how well students interact with others. Answer B is incorrect because hearing and vision screenings are important in helping to determine the cause of a student's struggles. Answer C is incorrect because many kindergarten students struggle with motor skills, which may impact their ability to learn.

89. D: He goes out of his way to annoy others, is defiant, and goes into childish rages in which he blames others. This student has been diagnosed with oppositional defiant disorder, a psychiatric disorder characterized by noncompliance, tantrums, extremely irritating conduct, refusal to follow rules, argumentative behavior, and blaming others.

90. D: Boys are identified with learning disabilities at a higher rate than girls but not likely because expectations are higher for girls. Although some teachers may have biases and expectations for girls and boys, there is no evidence to suggest that this had led to underidentifying girls. It is, however, important to identify students for special education evaluations for the right reasons. Answers A and B are incorrect because boys tend to exhibit more negative behaviors in the classroom than girls, and these can lead to special education referrals. Answer C is incorrect because some assessment tools are more sensitive to learning profiles more typical of boys.

91. B: Manipulatives make the abstract concepts of mathematics more concrete for students, making them good choices for students whose levels of cognitive development allow more concrete than abstract thought. Historically they have been physical objects, but, this is no longer necessary with computer technology (A). Virtual manipulatives are available and are also found effective (C). For example, the University of Utah has developed (and continues to develop) the National Library of Virtual Manipulatives through a grant from the National Science Foundation. While students cannot handle virtual manipulatives like physical ones, they can still view and manipulate objects onscreen to see concept relationships and applications more concretely. These virtual programs are interactive and promote students' active engagement more than traditional math lessons typically do (D).

92. C: Although all of these choices can be beneficial in supporting students like Max, it is important to distinguish the difference between accommodations and supplementing his curriculum. Providing opportunities for him to experience hands-on learning can be beneficial in allowing him to feel the numbers and improve his math. Accommodations are tools that allow him to access the same curriculum as his peers. Answer A is incorrect because although reading problems to him orally is beneficial, this is an accommodation to the general education curriculum. Answer B is incorrect because allowing him extra time would not supplement the curriculum. Answer D is incorrect because allowing him to use a computer can be helpful for an alternative curriculum or accommodation but not necessarily to supplement the curriculum.

93. C: For students with learning disabilities in the area of math, it is important to break down their learning to demonstrate how everything fits together. If they struggled with the previous lesson, they may need some additional instruction before they can move on to the next lesson. It is important that they are instructed at a speed and level that meet their needs and ensure that there is a smooth transition between topics. Answer A is incorrect because simply providing students with learning disabilities with more information may overwhelm them. Answer B is incorrect because ensuring that they understand the curriculum will likely occur as the lesson is being taught and not before. Answer D is incorrect because it may not be appropriate to challenge these students while learning is still occurring.

94. D: Although there may be many benefits to holding an externally facilitated IEP meeting, it typically takes a little longer for the special education teacher to prepare. The purpose of the externally facilitated IEP meeting is to include everyone in the conversation using an outside facilitator who may or may not know the student. The external facilitator will need to meet with the special education teacher beforehand in order to get an understanding of the student, which tends to take extra time. Answer A is incorrect because the facilitated IEP meeting is designed to be focused and handle one issue at a time. Answer B is incorrect because part of the facilitator's role is to ensure that they can problem solve whenever a conflict does arise. Answer C is incorrect because everyone on the IEP team will be included in the discussion at a facilitated IEP meeting.

95. B: One of the most effective ways that special education teachers can support the parents of students with disabilities is to make sure that they stay informed. Holding meetings regularly on different topics can give the parents the tools they need to make their own decisions on what might be best for their child. This can also give them an opportunity to speak to other parents with disabled children to discuss strategies that they have used. Answer A is incorrect because just giving them a list of facts likely wouldn't be as meaningful as holding meetings in which they can ask questions. Answer C is incorrect because having them come in to shadow their son likely wouldn't help them with strategies they can use at home. Answer D is incorrect because it can be tricky to give them a list of providers without knowing their financial and healthcare situations.

96. A: Special education classrooms, once attended throughout the day by students with disabilities, are being used less frequently. Many students with disabilities are now in regular classrooms and may only spend a portion of their time in a special education classroom. This is also true for students with learning disabilities. Depending on the severity of the disability, a student may visit the special education room for a short period of time each day to receive additional support in his or her area of weakness. English and math are the most common subjects that students go to special education classrooms to receive instruction or help in.

97. A: According to IDEA, birth trauma would not be considered one of the causes of traumatic brain injury. Students with birth trauma would likely be considered under a different eligibility category. Students who receive services under the traumatic brain injury category will typically have a medical diagnosis of a traumatic brain injury. Answer B is incorrect because combat injuries can be one of the causes of traumatic brain injuries, even at a young age. Answer C is incorrect because violence is often associated with students who are impacted by traumatic brain injuries. Answer D is incorrect because sports-related injuries can also cause damage to the brain and cause traumatic brain injuries.

98. C: Standardized tests are fairly accurate if given to typical American students. But Fernando is not a typical American child and should not have been given the same tests. Therefore option A is incorrect.

It is true that a lack of formal schooling creates a disadvantage on standardized tests. But this is not the most glaring factor in this case. Fernando's rural background, while contributing, did not influence his test scores as much as the fact that he is not a native English speaker. Therefore option B is incorrect.

Fernando and his parents speak Spanish at home. Newly arrived in the USA, they do not know much English. From this it should be obvious (though administrators missed or ignored it) that testing this child with standardized measures for English-speaking students was inappropriate. He needs sufficient ESL or ELL instruction before he can perform successfully on such tests. Therefore option C is correct.

Fernando could be disoriented by the move to a different culture and this could interfere with testing. But it is not as big a reason for his lower performance as his lack of English language skills. Therefore option D is incorrect.

99. B: Derrick can only use one arm and hand, so assembly of small machine parts would be difficult and frustrating. Therefore, option A is incorrect.

Sorting small machine parts is more appropriate. Derrick's eyesight is good, so he can identify differences in shapes. He can pick up and place parts in separate containers with one hand. Therefore, option B is correct.

Assembly line work could involve standing up, but Derrick is in a wheelchair. It would also likely involve using both arms and hands, and it would probably require physical stamina and movement beyond Derrick's capabilities. Therefore, option C is incorrect.

Requisitioning and ordering parts would involve reading and writing. With profound intellectual disabilities, Derrick would be unable to do these things. In addition to filling out forms, this job could also involve speaking, which Derrick cannot do. Therefore, option D is incorrect.

100. D: Although removing the student from the school is certainly an option, this is not typically one of the dispute-resolution processes. These processes are designed for parents to work through disputes that they may have with their child's IEP in order to find a solution. Removing the student from the school likely would not solve the problem with regard to the IEP. Answer A is incorrect because parents and stakeholders have the right to file a complaint with the Department of Education if they choose to. Answer B is incorrect because asking for mediation can be a beneficial way to seek a compromise in regard to the IEP. Answer C is incorrect because parents can also file a due process complaint if the other two strategies prove to be unsuccessful.

Practice Test #2

1. Which of the following is NOT an accurate statement regarding teaching reading skills to students with learning disabilities?

a. Using both visual and auditory input greatly increases comprehension.
b. Using both visual and auditory input greatly increases reading speed.
c. Using both visual and auditory input distracts and confuses students.
d. Using both visual and auditory input works better than either alone.

2. Which of the following is *most* accurate about exceptional students who are gifted?

a. They typically have advanced social skills.
b. Their academic performance is superior.
c. Their IQ scores indicate their giftedness.
d. They typically have difficulty relating to peers.

3. Marissa is an 11th-grade student who accesses special education services as a student with autism spectrum disorder. Which of the following lesson plan elements would likely be most beneficial in meeting her needs in her math class?

a. Providing a cross-curricular curriculum
b. Providing multiple tasks to complete
c. Providing multiple choices
d. Providing hands-on instruction

4. Which of the following strategies is most effective in measuring the goals of students with behavior concerns?

a. Using curriculum-based measures
b. Comparing students to their peers
c. Counting the number of referrals
d. Using random time samples

5. Deaf parents who use American Sign Language (ASL) and want it to be their child's first language decide they want their child to attend general education school. Which of the following is NOT a duty of educators in the school?

a. To see that attending school does not interfere with the child's learning and mastery of ASL
b. To see that the child has opportunities in school to interact with others whose first language is also ASL
c. To see that the child spends equal time using ASL and spoken language
d. To see that aspects of the deaf culture are incorporated into the school's culture

6. Which of the following is the most appropriate use of technology to provide assistance with reading a story for a high school student who struggles with reading comprehension?

a. Allowing the student to use text-to-speech programs
b. Allowing the student to watch videos of the stories
c. Allowing the student to complete an online activity
d. Allowing the student to complete an electronic worksheet

7. When screening a student for potential deficiencies as a preschooler, which of the following would be considered typical emotional development?

a. Changing the rules of a game they play
b. Being rigid with daily routines
c. Wanting to be dependent on caregivers
d. Struggling to take turns with peers

8. Part of the emotional environment of a classroom is the relationships between the teacher and the children. Children learn and develop well in a nurturing relationship that includes all the following EXCEPT:

a. Consistency in the teacher's interactions with and expectations of the children
b. A firm emphasis on compliance with rules and routines
c. The empowerment of children with choices
d. The delivery of feedback in a positive manner

9. Which of the following is the most efficient and effective method for teaching word recognition to a class with a variety of student levels and needs?

a. Providing individualized direct instructions
b. Using multilevel teaching practices
c. Teaching to the class median
d. Creating smaller groups at each level

10. Which type of assessment compares a student's performance on a test to a national average for age/grade level?

a. Norm-referenced test
b. Criterion-referenced test
c. Performance-based test
d. Ipsative measure/test

11. Under IDEA, among legal rights and responsibilities of students, which of these is federal rather than varying by state or district?

a. Free, appropriate public education
b. Reporting dangerous behaviors
c. Advocating for policy changes
d. Peaceful dispute resolution

12. Who is always required by law to follow a student's IEP?

a. The school nurse
b. All school staff
c. Teachers who work with the student
d. No one is strictly required.

13. Mr. Campbell has several students in his class whose families are of lower socioeconomic status (SES). These students have been getting consistently lower grades and standardized test scores than the class average. These students are then transferred to Mr. Leon's class. Mr. Leon grew up with lower SES himself. In their new class, these students are getting grades and standardized test scores equal to the class average. What is the most likely reason for this?

a. Mr. Leon is biased in favor of these students because they have similar backgrounds.
b. Mr. Campbell was biased against these students out of a prevalent middle-class bias.
c. The students feel more comfortable in Mr. Leon's class, increasing their motivation.
d. The students were uncomfortable in Mr. Campbell's class and were underachieving.

14. In teaching basic mathematics, the following actions by teachers will benefit all students. However, which one is most likely to be needed more specifically for students with special needs in a general education classroom?

a. Carefully planning the coverage and order of instructional math content
b. Judicious selection and application of the specific instructional strategies
c. Designing practice activities that take a wide range of student needs into account
d. Giving intensive, direct instruction in mathematics to individual students

15. A kindergarten teacher has received a community outreach referral. She asks the school's speech-language pathologist to evaluate a preschool child for delayed language development, as the parents cannot afford to pay a private practitioner's fees. The parents bring their child to the school. The speech-language pathologist assesses the child and privately has a strong suspicion that this child is displaying many signs of early autism. The speech-language pathologist takes the appropriate action. What does she do?

a. Tells the parents what she suspects and recommends treatment
b. Refers the parents to a free community clinic for a complete behavioral assessment
c. Asks the referring kindergarten teacher to tell the parents that she suspects autism
d. Recommends that the parents take their child to their pediatrician for a checkup

16. A teacher has a student with dyscalculia who has trouble organizing addition and subtraction problems on paper. She can best help him by:

a. Encouraging memorization of number families. Committing them to memory is the only way.
b. Demonstrating a problem in different ways. Write a problem on the board: 11-3. Gather 11 books and take 3 of them away. Draw 11 Xs on the board and erase 3 of them.
c. Use graph paper to help him organize. Show him how to write the problems, keeping each number in a box aligned with other numbers.
d. Make a game of addition and subtraction problems. Divide the class into groups and let them compete to see which group can solve the most problems.

17. Which one of the following learning environments best allows for differentiated instruction?

a. Randomly placing the students with additional support needs throughout the classroom
b. Selectively placing the students with additional support needs throughout the classroom
c. Placing the students with additional support needs clustered together
d. Placing the students with additional support needs at the front of the class

18. Which of the following is the best example of an independent living skills goal for a high school student with a specific learning disability?

a. The student will be able to access the city bus.
b. The student will live with a roommate in an apartment.
c. The student will live in a group home.
d. The student will attend community college.

19. Which statement best explains why classroom centers or learning stations can support students with disabilities in particular?

a. They allow instruction to be differentiated with varied tasks, supports, and pacing based on individual needs.
b. They ensure students always have an opportunity one-on-one instruction from the teacher.
c. They allow the teacher to assign different versions of the same work to provide differentiated instruction on the same goals.
d. They allow for variation in the class routine and allow for students to interact with different peers.

20. Which assistive technology is LEAST applicable to difficulties with writing?

a. A computer's keyboard
b. Speech-to-text software
c. Text-to-speech software
d. Using graphic organizers

21. Which of the following best supports differentiated instruction?

a. Lecturing in a clear voice and using simple language
b. Assigning the same essay to all students
c. Offering a choice of an essay, presentation, or video for the final project
d. Bringing in guest speakers of various nationalities

22. Madison is a third-grade student who receives special education services due to a hearing impairment. Which of the following special service providers would be LEAST likely to attend her reevaluation meeting?

a. Speech-language pathologist
b. Occupational therapist
c. School nurse
d. District audiologist

23. Which of the following is the best example of how a lifelong skill can be appropriately implemented into a lesson plan for high school students with disabilities?

a. Incorporating the stock market into a math lesson for students with Down syndrome
b. Incorporating newspaper reading into an English lesson for students with ADHD
c. Incorporating budgeting skills into a math lesson for students with learning disabilities
d. Incorporating creative writing into an English lesson for students with autism

24. Which of the following is true about stakeholder rights and an Independent Educational Evaluation (IEE)?

a. The testing is administered by someone who is not employed by the school district.
b. The IEP team must accept the results of the IEE.
c. The parents must pay for the IEE to be conducted.
d. The parents must explain the reason for the IEE.

25. What impact did the No Child Left Behind Act of 2001 have on school funding and English learners?

a. Schools must measure and share student results, including those of English learners, on state standardized tests to receive federal funds.
b. Schools should not include English learners in their school results for state standardized tests to receive funding.
c. All classes must have English learners to receive federal funding so that they are integrated into mainstream classes.
d. Schools must offer all state standardized tests to English learners in the language of their choice and report that to the state.

26. Which of the following best describes how the results of an intelligence test can guide instruction?

a. To determine whether a student qualifies for special education services
b. To determine whether a student has an emotional disability
c. To determine which accommodations students should access
d. To determine whether a student has a learning disability

27. Which of the following would be the most appropriate for a student who was evaluated for special education services and provided accommodations, but was later found to not have a disability?

a. Referring the student back to general education without accommodations
b. Referring the student back to general education with accommodations
c. Referring the student to the 504 team
d. Referring the student to supports outside of school

28. Jessica is a ninth-grade student who struggles with becoming distracted while she works in the general education setting. Which of the following methods of differentiated instruction would be most beneficial to Jessica?

a. Differentiating the learning environment
b. Differentiating the content
c. Differentiating the process
d. Differentiating the product

29. In facilitating reading comprehension and critical thinking in students with disabilities, which of the following strategies is best for visualizing concepts?

a. Teaching summarization
b. Using graphic organizers
c. Using multiple strategies
d. Teaching story structure

30. In the table below are several test scores for the same individual student, Mario.

Z-SCORE	STANDARD SCORE	SCALED SCORE	T-SCORE	PERCENTILE
3.70	155	20	87	99.99

Based on this table, which of the following is correct?

a. These must be scores Mario got on several different tests.
b. Mario scored much higher in some areas of a test than others.
c. If these are IQ scores, Mario must be a gifted student.
d. If these are IQ scores, Mario must have intellectual disabilities.

31. Which of the following best describes the implications for teaching for those who follow the behaviorist learning theory?

a. The teacher communicates through positive or negative reinforcements.
b. The teacher provides an environment that promotes self-learning.
c. The teacher facilitates collaborative learning and group work.
d. The discovery of students' behavior is guided by the teacher.

32. Rob is a second-grade student with a hearing impairment. Which of the following characteristics would not be included in the criteria for his continued eligibility?

a. His hearing impairment is fluctuating.
b. Amplification improves his hearing.
c. He also has a visual impairment.
d. His educational performance is adversely affected.

33. Gordon is a seventh-grade student with an intellectual disability. Which of the following is likely most important in ensuring that Gordon has a meaningful learning experience in the class?

a. Linking the content to real-life experiences
b. Making the content student-centered
c. Promoting self-knowledge
d. Using a variety of resources

34. Which of the following intervention strategies would be most effective in assisting a student who struggles to learn vocabulary terms?

a. Providing the student with a multisensory model
b. Supplying visuals with the words
c. Creating frequent vocabulary quizzes
d. Allowing students to use a dictionary

35. The school psychologist is explaining assessment results to Clifford's parents and other IEP team members. She says that Clifford has difficulties with planning, organizing, keeping track of time, and relating a current lesson to earlier learning. She also says that he talks out of turn in class. These all relate most to deficits in...

a. Executive function
b. Self-regulation
c. Sequencing
d. Memory

36. A student who has difficulty understanding spoken language has a deficit in:

a. Expressive communication
b. Receptive communication
c. Verbal communication
d. Social communication

37. A teacher has a child who does not volunteer in class. When the teacher asks the student a question the student can answer, she does so with as few words as possible. The teacher isn't sure how to best help the child. She should:

a. Leave the child alone. She is clearly very shy and will be embarrassed by having attention drawn to her. She is learning in her own way.
b. Ask two or three highly social children to include this girl in their activities. She is shy, and she probably won't approach them on her own.
c. Observe the child over the course of a week or two. Draw her into conversation and determine if her vocabulary is limited, if she displays emotional problems, or if her reticence could have another cause. Note how the child interacts with others in the class. Does she ever initiate conversation? If another child initiates, does she respond?
d. Refer her to the school counselor immediately. It is clear the child is suffering from either a low IQ or serious problems at home.

38. Joseph is a fourth-grade student being evaluated for special education services as a student with a specific learning disability in the area of math problem solving. Which of the following would be the best interpretation of his assessment results that show he is within one standard deviation of the mean in math problem solving?

a. Joseph would likely be determined eligible for special education services.
b. Joseph would likely need more testing in order to determine his eligibility.
c. Joseph would likely be determined ineligible for special education services.
d. Joseph would likely be determined eligible for a 504 Plan instead.

39. The ABC approach to behavior analysis stands for...

a. Alphabetical classifying
b. Analysis brings changes
c. Appropriate behavioral choices
d. Antecedent-behavior-consequence

40. Behavioral management should include specific techniques for students who have difficulty staying on task. Which one of the following would NOT be appropriate?

a. Allowing such students to walk around to look at the materials that pertain to the lesson
b. Assigning specific tasks to be completed
c. Using response cards so that all students feel compelled to be aware and involved
d. Not allowing peer helpers because they might harm more than help by distracting the students who have trouble staying on task

41. Which one of the following is the best example of a culturally responsive special education classroom?

a. Acknowledging ethnic holidays and celebrations
b. Pairing students with similar backgrounds
c. Incorporating texts from various cultures
d. Showing popular films that feature other cultures

42. A teacher suspects one of her kindergarteners has a learning disability in math. Why would the teacher suggest intervention to the child's concerned parents rather than assessment as the first step?

a. She wouldn't; assessment should precede intervention
b. She wouldn't; kindergarteners develop new skills at radically different rates. Suggesting either intervention or assessment at this point is premature. The teacher would more likely observe the child over a three month period to note her development before including the parents about her concern
c. Assessing a young child for learning disabilities often leads to an incorrect conclusion because a student must be taught the subject before it's possible to assess her understanding of it. Intervention teaches the child specific skills to correct her misconceptions. If the intervention fails, assessment is the next step
d. Assessment at this stage is unnecessary and wastes time and money. Since an assessment that resulted in a diagnosis of a learning disability would recommend intervention to correct it, it is more efficient to proceed directly to intervention

43. Among the following, a child with which type of disability is likely to be best at focusing attention on one thing for a long time?

a. Down syndrome
b. Developmental delay
c. Attention-deficit/hyperactivity disorder
d. Autism spectrum disorder

44. Joel lived for many years at an institution and has now been placed in a group home. He has profound intellectual disabilities and a number of obsessive-compulsive behaviors. He has certain habits; for example, at meals he tends to sit sideways at the table with his legs crossed, with the result that he drops a great deal of food on the floor. What should the houseparent do?

a. Put Joel in a time-out for the rest of the meal when this occurs.
b. Direct Joel to clean up the floor after the meal is over.
c. Meet with Joel's IEP team to write training objectives.
d. Place a drop cloth on the floor under Joel's chair.

45. Which of the following best describes the goal of implementing a functional curriculum for students with disabilities?

a. To teach independent living skills to students
b. To teach communication skills to students
c. To teach basic subjects to students
d. To teach everyday tasks to students

46. Which of the following classroom climate factors is most important when working with at-risk learners with disabilities?

a. Allowing the students to access accommodations
b. Providing a caring classroom setting
c. Allowing these students to collaborate with peers
d. Providing opportunities for after-school activities

47. A special education teacher is working to create an IEP for one of her students. To complete her IEP, she needs to record when the student reached certain developmental and academic milestones. Who is the best person to reach out to in order to get this information?

a. The student's pediatrician
b. The student's previous teachers
c. The school counselor
d. The student's parent or guardian

48. Which of the following would be the best example of a learning objective that is appropriately challenging for a third-grade student with a disability in reading fluency?

a. The student will be able to identify 25 letters in one minute.
b. The student will be able to identify 25 letter sounds in one minute.
c. The student will be able to read 50 sight words in one minute.
d. The student will be able to read 100 words in one minute.

49. A student notices that a classmate, Karis, whom she has known for years, has become quiet and withdrawn from school. The original student approaches her math teacher to let her teacher know her concern. The teacher tells the student that Karis's mother has just died, and Karis is struggling to adjust. Which statement gives a correct assessment of the teacher's response to the student?

a. The teacher's response was ethical because she was stating facts about Karis, not opinions
b. The teacher's response was ethical because it allows the student to help Karis in a time of need
c. The teacher's response was unethical because Karis should be present for this conversation
d. The teacher's response was unethical because it violated Karis' right to confidentiality

50. Sammy is blind and deaf and has spent his preschool, kindergarten, and first and second grade years in a special school for blind and deaf students. He has been very successful as a student. Because of his success and his family's relocation to another city, he has been recommended for placement in a general education school. Who should be involved in designing and implementing transition plans?

a. Sammy's former teacher and his new teacher
b. Sammy's new teacher and his parents
c. Sammy's former teacher, new teacher, and parents
d. Sammy's parents, former and new teachers, and Sammy

51. Annie is a student with severe intellectual disabilities, a personality disorder, and a history of maladaptive behavior, including tantrums, self-injury, aggression, and property destruction. One day, behavioral staff members are on a field assignment and not present at the school when Annie has a major tantrum. A teacher reports the incident to them when they return. Which of the following would the staff likely have employed had they been there?

a. Proactive strategies during tantrum escalation
b. Reinforcement during tantrum escalation
c. Proactive strategies before the tantrum could escalate
d. Proactive strategies during the tension reduction phase

52. Which of the following best describes the purpose of the Education for All Handicapped Children Act of 1975?

a. To mandate free appropriate public education for students with disabilities
b. To provide grants to states to fund special education programs
c. To establish services to facilitate school-to-work transitions
d. To allow students with disabilities to be included in statewide assessments

53. Ms. Winslow has a class with many students with learning disabilities (LD). She consistently calls her students' attention to features in their textbooks such as boldface headings, illustrations, tables, charts, indexes, and chapter summaries. Which is most accurate regarding this practice?

a. Doing this helps her students to organize what they read and learn.
b. She does this because her students don't read textbooks.
c. It enhances her presentation but does not really facilitate learning.
d. This helps her LD students but is a waste of time for other students.

54. Before being assigned to a special education classroom, a student must:

a. Agree to the reassignment.
b. Have an Individualized Education Program developed.
c. Have a Section 504 plan developed.
d. Be seen by an educational psychologist to confirm diagnosis.

55. Marie is a fifth-grade student who receives special education services as a student with a hearing impairment. Which of the following sections in the IEP describes the support that Marie will receive specific to her disability?

a. Communication plan
b. Annual goals
c. Accommodations
d. Special factors

56. Which of the following is NOT usually required as a component of an IEP?

a. Accommodations
b. Objectives
c. Annual goals
d. Present levels

57. Ms. Malone, who teaches in an elementary school, is informed that her class will include five students who have cerebral palsy this year. Of these five, two also have diagnoses of intellectual disabilities. Ms. Malone can expect that:

a. All five students will have very similar degrees of disability due to their cerebral palsy.
b. The two students with intellectual disabilities will have much greater special education needs than the three with only cerebral palsy.
c. The magnitude of the special education needs of the two students with intellectual disabilities should depend solely on their levels of intellectual disabilities.
d. The degrees of disability and special education needs of all five students could vary widely.

58. When does special education law apply to LEPs?

a. Never; the two are distinct and share no overlap.
b. Only when an LEP student also has learning, emotional, or physical disabilities as well
c. Always
d. It has not been definitively decided.

59. For an incoming student from a different culture, which of the following characteristics has the greatest impact on the identification of special education needs?

a. The language the student speaks
b. The content the student has learned
c. The location the student comes from
d. The religion the student practices

60. What is not included in an Individual Education Plan?

a. Medical issues or information
b. The student's interests
c. Family history of disability
d. Test results

61. Rachel teaches in a resource room with students of various ages and different grade levels. One student, Peter, has mastered addition, subtraction, multiplication, and short division. He is just beginning long division. Joe is a year older, has mastered long division, and is working on fractions. How could Rachel apply Vygotsky's principle of the zone of proximal development with these two students?

a. Have Peter and Joe both do Joe's fraction problems together to accelerate Peter's progress.
b. Have Peter and Joe split the work and do Peter's long division problems together to give Peter confidence.
c. Have Joe help Peter with long division, as Joe is just slightly more advanced than Peter is.
d. Have each student work long division problems separately and compare their answers.

62. Having a print-rich environment includes all of the following EXCEPT:

a. Writing classroom labels in only one language to avoid confusion
b. Making sure print is at the children's eye level
c. Displaying the students' work around the classroom
d. Having the teacher prepare materials in front of the students to model writing

63. A kindergarten teacher is showing students the written alphabet. The teacher pronounces a phoneme, and one student points to it on the alphabet chart. The teacher is presenting:

a. Letter-sound correspondence
b. Rote memorization
c. Predictive analysis
d. Segmentation

64. Which of the following is the best example of guided practice when supporting a fifth-grade general education social studies class with multiple students with disabilities?

a. Students independently complete a map worksheet.
b. Teachers provide feedback on the map worksheet.
c. Students work in small groups to complete the map worksheet.
d. Teachers model how to complete the map worksheet.

65. Donna is a speech therapist who has just moved to a new school. She inherits a caseload from the previous person who was not a speech therapist but a general education teacher with some course credits in special education. She discovers that one student, Erin, has been placed in a special education classroom with other "speech therapy students." However, the other students in this group all have delayed language development, whereas Erin stutters. Erin reads and writes above grade level, has a high IQ score and a large vocabulary, and gets good grades in all subjects. What action should Donna take?

a. Keep Erin in the same group but also does a lot of one-on-one stuttering therapy with her.
b. Find two other students who stutter and form a new group with them and Erin.
c. Advocate for Erin to be in the general classroom with speech therapy sessions.
d. Work individually with Erin, as her stutter would humiliate her in the classroom.

66. The ADA is:

a. The Americans with Disabilities Act
b. The Anti-Discrimination Act
c. The American Diabetes Association
d. The Alternatives to Discrimination Act

67. William is autistic and is very proficient at computer programming. His teacher helped him to find a part-time computer job while he was still in high school. William has always lived at home with his parents. He will be attending community college classes following graduation from high school and continuing to work at his part-time job. He is interested in living on his own but is unsure about what he will need to know to accomplish this. How might his teacher best help him reach this goal?

a. Advise him to take a class in independent living skills along with his other classes.
b. Tell him about a free resource network's website that helps people make such transitions.
c. Tell him to try getting an apartment with a roommate and see how he likes it.
d. Advise him to stay at home with his parents until he is more prepared to move.

68. A ninth grade special education teacher is giving students strategies for taking a Maze test. There will be several paragraphs in which some words have been blanked out. There are five possible answers for each blank. The best approach is to:

a. Read all answers; mark out any that are illogical. 'Plug in' the remaining words and mark out those that are grammatically incorrect or do not sound right using context clues.
b. Read the first answer first. If it is logical and sounds grammatically correct, select that word and move on to the next question. If not, move to the second answer and repeat.
c. Cover the answers and try to guess what the correct word is. Look at the five choices. Select the one closest in meaning to the word guessed.
d. Do the questions that seem easier first. Look for a pattern and select the remaining words accordingly.

69. Which of the following best describes when it would be appropriate to provide one-on-one in-class support to a fifth-grade student who receives special education services and has been demonstrating an inability to attend to his general education teachers?

a. As soon as the student demonstrates these behaviors
b. At the student's annual IEP meeting
c. After data have been collected and analyzed
d. When the student gets suspended from school

70. According to the Individuals with Disabilities Education Act (IDEA), which condition could fall under the umbrella term of specific learning disability?

a. Speech or language impairment
b. Auditory processing disorder
c. Attention deficit disorder
d. Bipolar disorder

71. Which of the following is the primary benefit of using small-group pull-out instruction to provide IEP accommodations for high school students with disabilities?

a. Providing students access to their IEP accommodations
b. Allowing the students to ask questions
c. Reducing teacher workload by focusing instruction
d. Providing extra practice with reading, writing, and math

72. Which of the following is an instructional strategy that is LEAST likely to be effective when working with a group of sixth-grade students with ADHD?

a. Offering choices of task completion to the students
b. Providing hands-on learning activities
c. Providing a task above the students' current skill level
d. Repeating instructions often throughout the task

73. Jaden is a second-grade student with a diagnosis of ADHD. When conducting a special education evaluation, which of the following behavior rating scales would be most appropriate?

a. Observer/informant scales
b. Self-report scales
c. Peer scales completed by classmates
d. Self-monitoring checklists

74. What legislation gives students and families increased protection in regard to the confidentiality of student records?

a. No Child Left Behind Act
b. Americans with Disabilities Act
c. Family Educational Rights and Privacy Act
d. Human Equity Act

75. Which of the following would be the LEAST appropriate for a special education teacher to use to evaluate the progress of their students on their IEP goals?

a. Standardized assessment data
b. Curriculum-based assessments
c. Classroom observations
d. End-of-quarter grades

76. Laws and ethics are important areas of concern for the classroom teacher, starting with an understanding of the differences between laws and ethics. Of the following statements, which one is FALSE?

a. Laws are concrete, written, and enacted by people.
b. Ethics are less tangible and observable and consist of ideas.
c. Laws are always ethical.
d. Most laws are the codification of what society considers moral or ethical obligations.

77. What can a teacher do in regard to the physical environment of the classroom to increase attention and learning?

a. Cover every wall with posters
b. Play music
c. Ensure the class is brightly lit
d. Arrange the desks in a circle

78. Jeanine is a ninth-grade student who often disrupts class with outbursts when she doesn't get her way. Which of the following would be the LEAST effective way to respond to her behavior when this occurs?

a. Ignore the behavior and continue class
b. Calling for backup
c. Negotiating with her
d. Removing her from class

79. Which of these is true regarding the relationships between state agencies and local health departments?

a. Each state has a centralized structure, and the state agency controls local public health services.
b. Each state is decentralized, letting local health departments make decisions and deliver services.
c. Each state has mixed/shared authority, with a combination of centralized and decentralized structure.
d. Some states are centralized, some are decentralized, and some have mixed/shared authority.

80. Which of the following would be the greatest disadvantage of co-teaching?

a. One teacher may teach more than the other.
b. The teachers may disagree on strategies.
c. The teachers may not be experts in certain subjects.
d. One of the teachers may not have much experience.

81. Cheyenne is an eighth-grade student with an OHI due to a heart condition, and she struggles with attendance. Which of the following would be the best example of a weekly objective in assisting Cheyenne in getting caught up?

a. Cheyenne will talk to each of her teachers at the beginning of each week.
b. Cheyenne will meet with her case manager to develop a plan for getting caught up.
c. Cheyenne will come in before school to talk to her teachers.
d. Cheyenne will complete all her missing assignments by the end of the week.

82. Which of the following instructional strategies would be most appropriate when teaching a science lesson to a third-grade class?

a. Reciprocal teaching
b. Socratic questioning
c. Direct instruction
d. Learning centers

83. Which of the following is a metacognitive learning strategy that aids in transferring learning to new, real-world situations?

a. Repetition
b. Learning to learn
c. Memorization
d. Passive listening

84. Jimmy is a general education eighth-grade student who is starting to struggle in the area of math calculations. Which of the following is the next step for his teacher?

a. Referring Jimmy for special education services
b. Attempting accommodations inside the classroom
c. Contacting Jimmy's parents about getting a tutor
d. Offering to work with Jimmy after school

85. Which of the following is most accurate regarding grouping strategies for teaching disabled and diverse students using multilevel instructional techniques?

a. These are best taught to the whole class.
b. Small groups are the optimal arrangement.
c. Multilevel instruction is best used in pairs.
d. A range of grouping strategies can be used.

86. As defined by the Individuals with Disabilities Education Act (IDEA), Secondary Transition is a coordinated set of activities that are:

a. Results-oriented and include post-school activities, vocational education, employment support and adult services and considers the individual's strengths, preferences and interests
b. Socially structured and consider the individual's strengths, preferences and interests and vocational requirements
c. Designed to support vocational training, results-oriented and have a strong social component
d. Selected by the parent(s) or guardian because the student cannot choose for himself

87. A young boy in the first grade is struggling to stay on task and keep his body under control during class. His constant movements are distracting other students and keeping him from completing the day's work. How should the situation be handled in the classroom?

a. Sit with him and break down the day's work into smaller segments. Help him alternate between physical activities just outside the classroom (such as jumping jacks or running errands in the hallway) and completing his segmented activities for the day.
b. Agree upon a nonverbal signal. When the signal (clearing the throat, touching the nose) is given, the boy is reminded to sit down and focus on his work.
c. Call his name sharply in class to get his attention. Clearly communicate the expectations for behavior and work completion so that he knows what he should be doing.
d. Call his parents to discuss the problem. Suggest having him evaluated for certain learning difficulties so that all adults involved in his care can work together to help him.

88. Which one of the following is NOT typically used to collect data as a curriculum-based assessment?

a. DIBELS
b. AIMSweb
c. EasyCBM
d. TerraNova

89. A resource room teacher has a small group of second and third graders who are struggling with reading comprehension. The most effective strategy would be to:

a. Present a list of vocabulary words before students read a particular text.
b. Ask students to create a play about the story.
c. Read a story aloud. Ask students to raise their hands when they hear an unfamiliar word.
d. Have each child keep a book of new vocabulary words. Whenever an unfamiliar word is seen or heard, the student should enter the word in this personal dictionary.

90. When working with a group of students that struggle with study skills, which instructional strategy would be the MOST effective?

a. Group discussion
b. Independent practice
c. Portfolio development
d. Cooperative learning

91. Which of the following is not considered a disability category according to IDEA?

a. Multiple disabilities
b. Developmental disabilities
c. Intellectual disabilities
d. Orthopedic impairment

92. A student with disabilities does not demonstrate certain adaptive life skills such as cleaning up a work area at school, but his parents report that he has done so at home for years. An ecological assessment finds he does not demonstrate these skills in any other settings. Which instructional procedure is most appropriate for this student?

a. Reteaching him these skills
b. Teaching skill generalization
c. Teaching skill maintenance
d. Teaching skill discrimination

93. Ms. George has some new students in her special education class this year. After she has assigned individual seatwork, she notices that two Chinese girls are helping each other. What should she do?

a. She should punish them for cheating and tell them to do the assignment over individually.
b. She should acknowledge potential cultural factors and explicitly teach classroom expectations.
c. She should separate the girls' seats so they can continue seatwork but not work together.
d. She should report their activity to the school principal and let her address it with the girls.

94. Corey is a third-grade student with a specific learning disability in the area of reading fluency. Which of the following assessments would be most appropriate in determining his eligibility for special education services?

a. Wechsler Preschool and Primary Scale of Intelligence
b. Wechsler Individual Achievement Test
c. Wechsler Intelligence Scale
d. Wechsler Intelligence Scale for Children

95. Stewart is a student who uses a wheelchair. This year he will be placed in Ms. Joplin's class, where all the other students are ambulatory. He will be the only student in a wheelchair. Stewart's IEP team is meeting to discuss his placement. Regarding concerns about the wheelchair, what is the best recommendation?

a. Stewart should not be placed in this class, because his wheelchair will stand out, making both him and the other students feel uncomfortable about it.
b. Someone should accompany Stewart to transfer him from his wheelchair to a regular student desk/chair and then back to his wheelchair when it is time to leave the classroom.
c. Stewart should only be placed in a class that has other students who use wheelchairs.
d. School staff should ensure that the classroom is wheelchair-accessible and that Stewart can navigate it; they should also show other students how to adjust to the situation.

96. Which of the following is true?

a. Pre-service training is adequate preparation for the teachers to do their work
b. The school district is in the business of educating students, not teachers
c. Teachers should spend some of their work time in professional study and collaborative work
d. To avoid taking time away from students, teachers should pursue professional development on their own time

97. Aaron, a student in Mr. Love's class, has a diagnosis of attention-deficit/hyperactivity disorder. Aaron's mother has a history of some difficulties with compliance in giving Aaron his daily medication. Today Aaron does not remain on task for more than a few seconds at a time, and he does not stay in his seat for more than five minutes at a time. This is not typical of his daily behavior in the classroom. What should Mr. Love do?

a. Contact Aaron's doctor and recommend that his medication be reevaluated for a higher dose.
b. Contact Aaron's mother and ask whether she was able to give him his medication today.
c. Contact the school principal and recommend that Aaron be placed in a different classroom.
d. Contact Aaron's doctor and recommend that he be reevaluated for a different medication.

98. Which of the following is NOT a good practice to incorporate for students who have difficulty finishing routine assignments?

a. The teacher should teach self-discipline for staying on task.
b. The teacher should avoid incorporating games into the materials because they might add too much time to the task.
c. The teacher should remove segments of the task, such as requiring the student to copy word problems before calculating the answer.
d. The teacher should divide the task into segments and allow the student to work on the parts throughout the day.

99. What is true of an elementary school student's progress on his or her annual Individualized Education Program (IEP) goals, according to Individuals with Disabilities Education Act (IDEA)?

a. Parents are updated on progress once a year at the IEP meeting.
b. Parents are updated on progress weekly.
c. Parents are updated on progress as often as report cards are provided.
d. Parents are updated at the beginning and end of the school year.

100. Which of the following was one of the main purposes of the Individuals with Disabilities Education Act (IDEA) of 2004?

a. To create separate schools exclusively for students with disabilities
b. To protect the rights of students with disabilities
c. To afford students with disabilities protection from expulsion
d. To initiate new programming for students with disabilities

Answer Key and Explanations for Test #2

1. C: It is incorrect that using both visual and auditory input (C) distracts or confuses students with learning disabilities. The information is reinforced for them when presented in both sensory modalities. Special educators find that students' reading comprehension can improve dramatically when spoken language is presented along with printed language (A). They also find that students with reading learning disabilities, who typically read slowly and laboriously, can increase their reading speed just as dramatically when the auditory version is added to the visual (B). Therefore, it is correct that using visual and auditory input together is more effective than either sensory modality alone (D).

2. D: Some gifted students excel in all areas, including athletics and social skills (A), but not necessarily. Gifted children can have different abilities and interests than peers, making social interaction awkward. They may have difficulty relating to peers with more typical abilities and interests, resulting in peers who may not want to interact with them for being different. Some gifted children prefer academic/creative activities over social activities. Some gifted children show superior academic performance (B), while some do not. Some are bored by traditional curricula (including special education for the gifted) and lack motivation, while some use unconventional methods. As a child, Albert Einstein reportedly was failed in math by a teacher for achieving correct answers without following prescribed steps. Not all gifted children get high IQ scores (C) because giftedness also includes creativity or other forms not represented by IQ scores, not just intelligence. Some gifted children do not respond to standardized measures because they may think differently and/or be uninterested in test items.

3. D: Although all of these choices may be beneficial for students with autism, providing hands-on instruction would likely be the best option. It is important to provide different options for students to learn, especially those students who may struggle with the content. Giving students an opportunity to learn and demonstrate their knowledge using their hands can help them to retain the information. Answers A and C are incorrect because although cross-curricular connections and choices can be effective supports, they are less directly targeted to math concept acquisition than hands-on work in this context. Answer B is incorrect because giving a student multiple tasks might be difficult if they are struggling with the first task.

4. D: Although all these methods may be helpful in measuring a student's behavior needs, using random time samples can be beneficial in determining the frequency of the behavior. Random time samples allow teachers to observe the student at various times throughout the day to determine the cause and frequency of these behaviors. This can be measured to determine how much progress the student is making on their goals. Answer A is incorrect because curriculum-based measures tend to be more effective for students with academic goals. Answer B is incorrect because it may be difficult to measure how a student compares to their peers. Answer C is incorrect because simply counting the number of referrals likely does not provide sufficient data.

5. C: If ASL is the family's preferred language, and they choose attendance at a general education school, it is the job of teachers and administrators there to see that the education provided in this setting does not interfere with the child's use of his or her first language. Therefore, option A is incorrect.

It is also the duty of educators to see that the deaf child has opportunities within the school to communicate with others whose first language is also ASL. In a school that has a strong community involvement, it would even be encouraged that the school support interaction opportunities outside of explicit class time, such as through clubs or community events. Therefore, option B is incorrect.

When ASL is the first language of deaf children, the amount of oral language they are capable of using will vary. Whereas they will need some spoken language knowledge to communicate in a general education setting, having to use too much of it could interfere with their mastery of ASL, their first language. Using as much oral as sign language would also limit their communication if ASL is their first language. It is not the job of educators to see that the child spends equal amounts of time using both languages, and restricting the primary language of a child would be against the parents' desire. Therefore, option C is correct.

If the deaf parents want their child in an inclusive setting, it is the responsibility of educators to see that aspects of the deaf culture are incorporated into the school's overall culture. Therefore, option D is incorrect.

6. A: Although all of these examples may help students who struggle with reading comprehension, text-to-speech programs are best in allowing the student to access the curriculum. Text-to-speech programs provide students with reading comprehension problems the opportunity to listen to the same story that the rest of the class is reading. It is important to provide students access to the general education curriculum whenever possible. Answer B is incorrect because watching videos of the story won't always give them all of the information that they need in the story. Answer C is incorrect because an online activity may leave out some of what the rest of the class is doing. Answer D is incorrect because electronic worksheets may be more beneficial after the story has been read.

7. A: One of the typical emotional developments of a preschool student is playing games with friends or others. Children of this age will often start to change the rules of a game or make up their own rules to make it more fun or interesting. Recognizing the emotions of students during these social interactions is important in determining whether or not they are developing at the expected rate. Answer B is incorrect because being overly rigid and not wanting to change their routine or schedule is not usually considered typical of a preschool student. Answer C is incorrect because preschool students typically start to be less dependent on their caregivers during this time. While some issues with turn-taking may still be present in this age group, answer D is incorrect because children most often develop the ability to take turns without significant issues before entering preschool.

8. B: While setting rules and establishing routines is important to classroom management, the teacher should not be so firm that there is no room for flexibility and adjustments. A teacher's relationship with a child must remain consistent in terms of the teacher's interactions with the child and the expectations set for the child; a moody or fickle teacher can frustrate and anger the children. Teachers should respond to children positively and avoid negativity for the relationship to be constructive and nurturing. Although the teacher is the ultimate decision-maker in the classroom and must establish authority, sharing power with the children by guiding them into making responsible choices gives the children a sense of empowerment and a stake in the classroom situation.

9. B: Using multilevel teaching practices is an effective method to teach word recognition to a class of students with many reading levels and diverse needs. Giving direct instruction to individual students (A) is very effective but not efficient, and it can be impossible for one teacher to do this with typical class sizes. Creating smaller groups for each level (D) is similarly inefficient, as the teacher could end up with too many groups to teach in the time allowed. Teaching to the median (C) leaves out too many students who are below or above the medium range that the median targets. Multilevel practices address a variety of reading levels and allow adaptations for special student needs.

10. A: Norm-referenced tests compare the student's score to norms, such as national averages of scores for students of the same age or grade level. These are standardized tests, such as national achievement tests including the SAT, ACT, GRE, etc. Criterion-referenced tests (B) do not compare students' scores to other students' scores, but rather measure students' performance against a criterion, standard, or objective previously determined and given to students before testing. Class quizzes, exams, oral reports, presentations, experiments, and performance-based tests (C) are examples of criterion-referenced tests. Ipsative measures or tests (D) compare the student's performance to their own previous performance.

11. A: A free, appropriate public education (in the least restrictive environment possible) is a federal right guaranteed to students with qualifying disabilities under the IDEA. Reporting dangerous behaviors (B) to school staff is a student responsibility that varies by state or school district. Student rights to advocate for changes in policy (C) or law and to peaceful dispute resolution (D) also vary by state or district.

12. C: By law, all teachers working with a particular student must follow that student's Individualized Education Plan. Information contained within an IEP is confidential and is only available to faculty and staff who have a valid educational interest in the student. Therefore, the school nurse and other school staff are not necessarily required to follow an IEP, only those who are directly responsible for implementing any part of the student's IEP.

13. B: Based on research findings, it is highly likely that Mr. Campbell was subject to the middle-class bias prevalent among middle-class teachers. Many lower-SES students appear to achieve less, but teacher expectations often have more influence on these results than student ability and/or performance. Therefore, option B is correct.

Because Mr. Leon came from a lower-SES background, he may identify with these students, but this does not necessarily mean he would inflate their grades. Applying insights from his own experience, he might just as likely avoid special favors, hoping to ensure the students' hard work and success in middle-class society. Therefore, option A is incorrect.

Undoubtedly these students feel more comfortable with Mr. Leon, and this could increase their motivation to succeed. But this is not the only reason for the difference. Their increased comfort and motivation may contribute to their improvement on objective measures but would not alone be enough to account for it. Removal of the middle-class bias would enable improved objective results and would also increase their comfort and motivation, which in turn could add to the improvement. Therefore, option C is incorrect.

These students probably did feel less comfortable with Mr. Campbell, but they may or may not have been underachieving in his class. The prevalence of middle-class bias among teachers would have an impact on their objective results regardless of the students' efforts. Therefore, option D is incorrect.

14. D: Carefully planning what the content of the math instruction covers and the order in which it is taught (A), using their best judgment in choosing and applying appropriate teaching strategies (B), and designing practice activities with a wide range of student needs in mind (C) are all actions by teachers that will improve the involvement and progress of all students, including those with special needs. The action most likely to be needed specifically by some special needs students in the general education classroom is using more intensive direct instruction methods to teach them basic mathematics.

15. B: Telling the parents what she suspects and recommending treatment without a formal diagnosis would be inappropriate. This speech language pathologist (SLP) is very observant and has a talent for diagnosis as well as being well-educated about and experienced with autism. And SLPs do work with some autistic individuals. Regardless of these things, she is not qualified to make such a diagnosis. This should be done by a licensed psychologist, behavior specialist, or psychiatrist. Telling the parents what she suspects could alarm them unnecessarily—especially if she turns out to be wrong or if a psychological practitioner disagrees and/or makes a different diagnosis. Therefore, option A is incorrect.

Referring the parents to a clinic for more thorough evaluation by qualified psychological personnel is the right thing to do. If her suspicions are confirmed, the diagnosis will be made by someone with credentials to back it up and who can recommend appropriate interventions. Referring to a free clinic is also helpful since the parents cannot afford to pay a private practitioner. Therefore, option B is correct.

Asking the referring kindergarten teacher to tell the parents is as inappropriate as telling them herself, since the teacher is also not qualified to make such a diagnosis. The SLP would also be evading personal responsibility by diagnosing outside of her role but using the teacher to deliver the information, which is not confirmed. Both actions would be unethical. Therefore, option C is incorrect.

Ruling out other physical or medical conditions is a good idea, and an astute physician may recognize early signs of autism just as the SLP did. But this step in itself is insufficient. To recommend a physical checkup and also refer the parents to a clinic for behavioral evaluation would be an acceptable action plan. Therefore, option D is incorrect.

16. C: Use graph paper to help him organize. Show him how to write the problems, keeping each number in a box aligned with other numbers. This will help him determine which numbers are in the ones group, the tens group, the hundreds group, and so on.

17. B: Although it may be easier in some aspects to have all of the students that need additional support together, this might create some issues. It is important to strategically place these students based on their needs and behavior. The teacher must be able to access these students in different ways that promote a safe and supportive classroom. Answer A is incorrect because randomly placing them could potentially create issues with their peers. Answer C is incorrect because if they are clustered together, they may feel singled out for being different from the other students. Answer D is incorrect because just putting them at the front could also isolate them.

18. A: Independent living skills goals focus on functional, teachable behaviors that support daily life after high school. Being able to access public transportation is a specific, measurable skill that can be taught and practiced. Answer B is incorrect because living with a roommate is a life outcome rather than a skill-based goal. Answer C is incorrect because living in a group home is a placement decision, not an instructional goal. Answer D is incorrect because attending community college is an educational outcome, not an independent living skill.

19. A: Classroom centers can be valuable for students with disabilities because they make it easier to differentiate instruction. Teachers can vary the task, materials, supports (e.g., visuals, sentence frames, manipulatives, assistive technology), pacing, and the way students show learning to match individual needs. Centers also allow the teacher to provide targeted small-group instruction while other students practice skills independently or collaboratively with clear routines. In addition to using learning centers to differentiate the instructional style, different learning stations can be used to help target different curricular objectives as students may have varied needs.

20. C: The technology least applicable to difficulties with writing is (C) text-to-speech software, which is used primarily to read text aloud and support students with reading or visual-access difficulties, rather than to support written expression. Students having problems with oral expression can type text, and the software converts it to synthesized speech. A computer's keyboard (A) is applicable to students who have difficulties with writing, but not with typing. It does not apply to students having equal trouble typing or writing, but is more applicable to longhand writing difficulties for students who can type. Using graphic organizers (D) is applicable because writing disorders commonly include problems with planning and organization, and graphic organizers facilitate these functions.

21. C: Because students learn in different ways, it is important to incorporate differentiated instruction in order to create the best learning environment for all students. This involves providing choice and changing content, product, process, or environment based on student needs. Choice C gives students the option to choose a project format that works best for them, so it is an example of differentiated instruction. Options A and B are undifferentiated, as they provide the same content in the same way to all students. While choice D could be beneficial in expressing diversity and connecting with students of various nationalities, it also provides the same content in the same manner to all students.

22. B: Although it is possible that the occupational therapist would provide services to a student with a hearing impairment, this is not typically the case. Occupational therapists often provide support to students who struggle with motor skills in the school setting. Students with hearing impairments may or may not have these needs, and it is important to understand the areas in which students have needs in order to consult with the appropriate service providers. Answer A is incorrect because speech-language pathologists typically assist students with hearing impairments in working on communication skills. Answer C is incorrect because the school nurse is an important member of the team in determining the health care services that the student may need at school. Answer D is incorrect because the audiologist typically conducts the hearing screening to determine the impact of the hearing impairment.

23. C: Students with learning disabilities will likely use budgeting when they enter adulthood and continue to use it throughout their entire life. This is an example of a skill that can be incorporated into a lesson plan for all students, including those with disabilities. It is crucial to teach students with disabilities skills that are appropriate for them and can be used throughout their lifetime. Answer A is incorrect because students with Down syndrome will most likely not deal with the stock market. Answer B is incorrect because being able to read a newspaper may or may not be a skill that students with ADHD use throughout their life, depending on their future career goals and interests. Answer D is incorrect because creative writing may benefit some students with autism, but it is not likely to be a lifelong skill for everyone.

24. A: When parents request an IEE, the testing must be administered by someone who is not employed by the school district. Parents have the right to request an IEE when they do not agree with the results of a special education evaluation. The school must consider the results of this evaluation in order to ensure that it is providing FAPE. Answer B is incorrect because although the IEP team must consider the results of the evaluation, they do not have to accept them. Answer C is incorrect because parents are not automatically required to pay for the IEE. When parents request an IEE, the district must either provide the IEE at public expense or request a due process hearing to defend its evaluation. Answer D is incorrect because an explanation is not required for the parents to request an IEE.

25. A: The No Child Left Behind Act of 2001 required that for schools to receive federal funding, they must measure and report student achievement on standardized tests for all students, including English learners. This includes state assessments. The Every Student Succeeds Act (ESSA), passed in 2015, gave states flexibility in how to measure and report achievement rather than using a prescribed measure from the federal government.

26. C: Although there are many uses for intelligence tests, determining which accommodations a student accesses can help guide instruction. Intelligence testing is important in determining the intellectual abilities of students. These results can reveal how accommodations may benefit them in the classroom and which ones would be the most appropriate for them to access. Answer A is incorrect because although an intelligence test can be helpful in determining whether or not a student has an intellectual disability, this does not alone determine whether a student qualifies for special education services. Answer B is incorrect because determining whether a student has an emotional disability would likely encompass more than just an intelligence test. Answer D is incorrect because learning disabilities are typically discovered through additional assessments as well.

27. A: If a student is evaluated for special education and later found not to have a disability, the school cannot continue providing the accommodations because eligibility requires documented evidence of a disability. Without such evidence, the student must return to the standard general education program. Answer B is incorrect because accommodations cannot legally be provided without a documented disability or a 504 plan. Answer C is incorrect because the student was found not to have a disability, and Section 504 requires a documented disability. Answer D is incorrect because referring students to outside supports is not necessary unless the evaluation indicates otherwise, which the prompt does not suggest.

28. A: In order for a student like Jessica to succeed in the general education setting, it is likely best to differentiate the learning environment. One way to do this would be to create a space in the classroom where there are no distractions. This way, Jessica can still access the content of her peers while being free from distractions that might impact her ability to learn. Answer B is incorrect because differentiating the content would not be appropriate; she can still learn what the other students learn. Answer C is incorrect because differentiating the process would not be appropriate; she can still learn the content in the same way that the other students learn. Answer D is incorrect because differentiating the product would not be appropriate; she can be assessed using the same methods as other students.

29. B: Graphic organizers depict ideas and information in a variety of ways, and all of them are visual (e.g., charts, maps, pictures, etc.). These can be very helpful to students with disabilities who have trouble comprehending abstract concepts or organizing information because they make the material more concrete by using another modality. Teaching students how to summarize (A) helps them identify the important points or themes in reading material, and teaching them how to analyze the structure of a story (D) aids reading comprehension while employing critical thinking. Both of these skills will not directly make information visual unless they are taught specifically using graphic organizers (which include semantic organizers/maps). Using multiple strategies (C) is always highly recommended, but such strategies may involve a range of modalities, not simply a visual one.

30. C: If these are IQ scores, Mario scored in the 99.99th percentile. This means he scored higher than all but 0.01% of the population. With an IQ score at the very top of the population, Mario would be considered gifted. Therefore, option C is correct.

These scores all express the same measures in different terms. Z-score, T-score, and scaled score express the same values as standard score, but they are based on a different numbering system. Based on the table's headings, these are not scores from different tests. Therefore, option A is incorrect.

Nothing in the table indicates that these scores represent different parts of a test. The table names different types of scoring methods. Therefore, option B is incorrect.

If these are IQ scores, Mario's score is higher than most of the population's. In addition to adaptive skills measures, the definition of intellectual disabilities is largely based on IQ scores. The mildest (highest IQ) level of intellectual disabilities corresponds to a range of IQ scores between 70 and 55. Mario's score is 155. Therefore, option D is incorrect.

31. A: The behaviorist learning theory states that the teacher teaches correct behaviors and the students understand them and apply them in the classroom. According to this theory, students learn these behaviors via positive and negative reinforcement. This is important in understanding which techniques and learning theories might be best for certain students as they learn. Answer B is incorrect because the behaviorist theory states that the student is shaped through reinforcement rather than self-learning. Answer C is incorrect because the teacher facilitating collaborative groups is an example of the constructivist learning theory. Answer D is incorrect because the teacher guiding students in understanding the environment is an example of the cognitivism theory.

32. C: According to IDEA, students with a dual diagnosis of a hearing and visual impairment are considered deaf-blind and receive services under that category. Students who have one diagnosis of a hearing impairment would be eligible under that category instead. It is important to understand each of the areas of impact for students so they can receive all of the services they are eligible for. Answer a is incorrect because students with fluctuating hearing can still be eligible for the "hearing impairment" category. Answer b is incorrect because amplification is expected to improve a student's hearing. Answer d is incorrect because if Rob's educational performance is adversely affected by his hearing loss, he would be eligible for the category.

33. A: Although all these strategies may be helpful in creating a meaningful learning experience for Gordon, connecting the content to real-life experiences can have the most value. Students with intellectual disabilities often learn best by practicing the content they learn rather than simply hearing about it. Because of this, applying what they learn will likely help them remember more for longer. Answer B is incorrect because simply making the content student-centered may not always provide meaning to these students. Answer C is incorrect because promoting self-knowledge would likely be a better strategy for students who can explore opportunities independently. Answer D is incorrect because simply having many resources may not necessarily provide much meaning.

34. B: Students tend to remember vocabulary words when they have some kind of visual to associate with the word. Many students that struggle with vocabulary words often need a lot of practice in understanding these new words, so giving them multiple methods to learn the words is beneficial. Simply telling the students what words to memorize often does not work with students with disabilities that struggle with vocabulary. Answer A is incorrect because providing a multisensory model may be helpful for some students but is not the most effective method of learning new vocabulary. Answer C is incorrect because additional vocabulary quizzes might become too overwhelming for some students. Answer D is incorrect because although a dictionary can help learn the term at first, this strategy will not likely be effective in the long term.

35. A: Executive function includes planning, organizing, keeping track of time, keeping track of multiple things, relating earlier learning to current learning, and other higher cognitive activities. Self-regulation (B) relates only to talking out of turn in class and is just one component of executive function. Sequencing (C) involves arranging items in the correct order (chronological, logical, etc.) and is also one specific aspect of executive function. Memory (D), or retaining and retrieving information, requires using mental strategies that are included in executive function.

36. B: A deficit in receptive communication is reflected by difficulty understanding the spoken language that one hears. Deficits in expressive communication (A) are reflected in difficulties with speaking. This may be related to language processing (as in difficulty retrieving words or constructing sentences) or speech (as in poor articulation, stuttering, or voice problems). Verbal communication (C) refers to using words vs. nonverbal communication such as gestures, body language, and facial expression, but this term does not differentiate between expressive and receptive communication. Social communication (D) is communication used in social interactions, but understanding spoken language is not limited to social interactions (it also occurs in classes, lectures, audio/video recordings, etc.).

37. C: Until the teacher monitors the child's verbal abilities and habits, she cannot determine if the lack of interaction suggests a learning disability, an emotional problem, or simply a shy personality. The teacher should informally observe the child over a period of time, noting if and when she initiates or responds to oral language, if she is reading with apparent comprehension, if her vocabulary is limited, and the degree to which the child is interested in understanding.

38. C: When students fall within one standard deviation of the mean, this is most often considered in the average range, and a student would not be eligible. Students being evaluated for a specific learning disability must have a score that is considered statistically significant in order to be eligible. It is important to understand where one standard deviation falls in order to determine where the student scores. Answer A is incorrect because the student would likely not be eligible unless they were outside one standard deviation. Answer B is incorrect because although it is possible that more testing could be considered, this score shows that the student is within the average range. Answer D is incorrect because there is likely not enough information to determine whether or not a 504 Plan would be appropriate for Joseph.

39. D: Antecedents are events that occur right before a problem behavior and can trigger the behavior. Consequences are events that occur right after a problem behavior and can reinforce the behavior. The ABC model of behavior analysis examines the sequence of an antecedent occurring, which then triggers the behavior, which is then reinforced by the consequence following the behavior. Knowing what precipitates the behavior, and what rewards it, helps to determine the behavior's function, or what it accomplishes for the individual.

40. D: Peer helpers are more likely to keep the restless student on task than to distract that student; therefore, peer helpers are a good idea. Allowing a student who has trouble staying on task to do a "gallery walk"; that is, to expend some energy by walking around to examine the lesson materials that are on display, is a good practice because once the student has seen the materials he or she is less likely to be distracted by wondering about them. A student who has trouble staying on task is helped by being assigned specific tasks to accomplish because breaking up the assignment into smaller jobs seems more achievable. Using response cards catches the attention of the student who has trouble staying on task and pulls that student into the lesson with the others.

41. C: Although all of these strategies may be beneficial at certain times, incorporating texts from various cultures allows students to learn about other parts of the world. It is a good idea to incorporate texts from some of the backgrounds of the students in the class as a way for others to learn more about that student. It is important to make those students from backgrounds that others may not know about feel comfortable in class. Answer A is incorrect because simply recognizing holidays does not necessarily teach students about that culture. Answer B is incorrect because pairing students with similar backgrounds does not teach the other students in the class. Answer D is incorrect because popular films can misconstrue certain aspects of a culture they feature, and showing films is not as immersive as reading a text can be.

42. C: Assessing a young child for learning disabilities often leads to an incorrect conclusion because a student must be taught the subject before it is possible to assess her understanding of it. Intervention teaches the child specific skills to correct her misconceptions. If the intervention fails, assessment is the next step. Because formal diagnoses of specific learning disabilities can be less reliable at very young ages, teachers typically begin with classroom interventions and progress monitoring, referring for a formal evaluation if concerns persist over time.

43. D: Children with autism spectrum disorder often have deficits in social skills, communication skills, and joint or shared attention. They tend to prefer focusing individual attention on one activity or subject for sustained periods and may have difficulty with transitions. Children with attention-deficit/hyperactivity disorder (C) have difficulty focusing and sustaining their attention, are easily distracted, and tend to jump from one thing to another. Children with intellectual disabilities secondary to Down syndrome (A) and those with overall developmental delays (B) are likely to have shorter attention spans and less ability to focus.

44. C: Joel has odd behaviors, but many can be remedied by training. A time-out is unlikely to change his behavior over the long term. Punishment is generally not the most effective method of changing behavior, especially if Joel has not yet been taught proper mealtime behavior; therefore, option A is incorrect.

Having Joel clean up the floor is another type of punishment. With an individual who has profound intellectual disabilities, this is unlikely to change his sitting and eating behavior; therefore, option B is incorrect.

The houseparent should meet with the IEP team to plan IEP objectives. The team can write objectives for Joel to sit facing forward with his legs under the table and to eat over the table. The behavior specialist can write a task analysis for the houseparent to implement in training him to perform these behaviors, with reinforcement of proper execution; therefore, option C is correct.

Placing a drop cloth under Joel's chair would make it easier for the houseparent to clean up after meals, but Joel will not learn anything. If he eats in other settings, he will still make a mess. If he learns to sit and eat properly at home, this will transfer to other places. It would be impractical and inappropriate to put a drop cloth under him wherever he eats; therefore, option D is incorrect.

45. A: Although all of these choices may be beneficial to students with disabilities, a functional curriculum is designed to teach students independent living skills. This curriculum typically replaces traditional secondary curriculum for certain students who may be candidates at the high school level. It tends to be designed for students who will struggle to live independently once they complete their schooling. Answer B is incorrect because although it may be helpful in developing communication skills, the sole purpose is not just for this communication development. Answer C is incorrect because functional curriculum is an alternative curriculum rather than teaching the basic subjects. Answer D is incorrect because the primary goal of functional curriculum is to teach independent living skills, not just to teach current everyday tasks.

46. B: Although all these choices can be helpful strategies for students who are at risk, providing a caring and supportive classroom environment is most likely to be effective. Many of these students do not have much positive support in their lives and need someone that they can trust and rely on. Although it may be difficult for these students to open up and talk, it is important that they have a caring classroom setting and someone that they can turn to when they need to talk. Answer A is incorrect because simply giving them accommodations may not provide them with enough support to be successful. Answer C is incorrect because requiring peer collaboration without a supportive climate may not be effective for students who are hesitant to engage. Answer D is incorrect because providing opportunities for after-school activities does not directly influence the classroom climate.

47. D: The parent/guardian is the best person to consult for this information. Parents and guardians have been with their children for their entire lives and would have much more information than any other source. They should have access to the student's medical records and will have information from before their children started attending school. Previous teachers and school counselors likely would not have access to most developmental milestones and would likely be missing other pertinent information.

48. D: In order to measure reading fluency, it is essential to provide a student with a reading passage and record how many words they can read in one minute. This can help to determine how much progress a student has made and what they may still need to work on. Reading fluency is an important skill for a third grader to practice each day by reading passages and developing a clear understanding of words. Answer A is incorrect because identifying letters is a skill that students typically work on before third grade. Answer B is incorrect because although identifying letter sounds can be important, it is not always the best indicator of reading fluency ability. Answer C is incorrect because although reading sight words can help with reading fluency skills, it is not a measure of reading fluency by itself.

49. D: When the teacher shared what was causing Karis' change in mood, she violated Karis's right to confidentiality. It is fine if Karis wants to share this information with other students, but that decision is not the teacher's to make. While the teacher can share this information with counselors or other school personnel who could potentially help Karis, it is not acceptable to share this information with students or other members of the community.

50. D: Both former and new teachers need to be involved in transition, but it should not be limited to them. Teachers should collaborate with all those who can contribute to planning. Therefore, option A is incorrect.

The second option omits Sammy's former teacher, who is a valuable source of information. Without his previous teacher's input, a good transition is not likely. Others are omitted as well. Therefore, option B is incorrect.

Both former and new teachers as well as Sammy's parents should definitely be included, so this option is closer to the ideal situation. However, it omits the student himself. Therefore, option C is incorrect.

The teachers, parents, and Sammy himself should all be included in transition planning. There are likely others who could also contribute to this planning. However, this option incorporates more of the people who should be included in planning than do the other three choices. Therefore, option D is correct.

51. C: Proactive strategies are used to prevent the escalation of behavior. If the behavior is already escalating, it is too late to apply such strategies, so option A is incorrect.

Reinforcement of any behavior strengthens the likelihood that the behavior will recur. The worst possible time to present reinforcement would be during the escalation of a tantrum. Doing so would increase the escalation and increase the odds of additional future tantrums; therefore, option B is incorrect.

Proactive strategies would be aimed at preventing the tantrum from escalating. These could redirect Annie's behavior and/or differentially reinforce other behavior, so option C is correct.

Tension reduction is the phase at the end of a tantrum, once the aggression, self-injury, and/or destruction are over. Typically, Annie would be crying, exhausted, and contrite at this stage. This would be far too late for proactive strategies. This would be a better time for support and debriefing; therefore, option D is incorrect.

52. A: The Education for All Handicapped Children Act of 1975 established that children with disabilities must be provided free appropriate public education (FAPE). This law became the basis for all special education funding and services through the federal government. The establishment of FAPE was important for students with disabilities and continues to be today. Answer B is incorrect because grants to states to fund special education programs had already been established prior to the passage of this act. Answer C is incorrect because school-to-work facilitation legislation was passed after 1975. Answer D is incorrect because the inclusion of all students with disabilities in statewide testing also occurred after the passage of this legislation.

53. A: The most accurate answer is choice A: Doing this helps Ms. Winslow's students to organize what they read and learn from the textbooks. While many of us are familiar with students never reading their textbooks (B), this is not Ms. Winslow's main reason for her practice. The textbook items she regularly points out to her students are all specific organizational devices. Thus, answer C is incorrect: This practice may or may not enhance her presentation, but it does facilitate learning. Answer D—that this helps students with learning disabilities but is a waste of time for other students—is also incorrect, since all students can benefit from being reminded to use these features in their textbooks as aids to effective learning.

54. B: An Individualized Education Program is a requirement of law. The plan, written by a team of individuals including the classroom teacher, the special education teacher, parents or guardians, the student (if appropriate), and other interested individuals, establishes objectives and goals and offers a timeline in which to reach them.

55. A: The communication plan is important for students with hearing impairments to describe the services that students like Marie will receive to access the curriculum. The communication plan describes the support available for students and the strategies that are used to communicate with others. The communication plan also lists the devices and assistive technology that these students may access. Answer B is incorrect because the annual goals describe which areas the student will focus on and be monitored in. Answer C is incorrect because the accommodations will list specific supports that will be put in place for the student to access the curriculum. Answer D is incorrect because the special factors section simply lists whether or not the student accesses the communication plan.

56. B: Although each one of these other components is required to incorporate into IEPs for students with disabilities, objectives are usually not required. Students will often have objectives that go along with their annual goals, but this is not a requirement for each student. Short-term objectives are required, however, for students who participate in alternative assessments aligned with alternate achievement standards. It is important to understand when and how to use objectives in an IEP and which students it may benefit. Answer A is incorrect because accommodations are essential in addressing how students will appropriately access the general education curriculum. Answer C is incorrect because annual goals are a required component of the IEP to determine what area the student will focus on. Answer D is incorrect because present levels are necessary to determine how much progress a student has made.

57. D: With cerebral palsy, the degree of disability can vary widely among individuals, so option A is incorrect.

A diagnosis of intellectual disabilities does not necessarily mean a student will have greater or lesser special education needs than those with only cerebral palsy. Their needs will depend on their individual abilities. For example, some students with cerebral palsy may have greater physical disabilities than some other students with both cerebral palsy and intellectual disabilities, so option B is incorrect.

While a student with mild intellectual disabilities may have a very different educational plan than a student with severe or profound disabilities, this does not necessarily mean that the lower-functioning students need a greater amount of intervention. They may have different assignments, different presentation modalities, and varying levels of difficulty, but they will not necessarily require more time or attention than higher-functioning intellectually disabled students. The level of severity is only one of many factors. For example, a student with mild intellectual disabilities and a higher IQ score could have more profound physical disabilities from CP than another student and thus require more adaptive devices and physical assistance, so option C is incorrect.

Since the degree of disability can vary widely among individuals with cerebral palsy and since the same is true of individuals with intellectual disabilities, option D is correct.

58. B: Special education law applies to LEPs only when the student also has learning, emotional, or physical disabilities. Under IDEA, only students with learning disabilities, emotional and/or behavioral disabilities, physical disabilities, and developmental disabilities are eligible for special services. LEP students typically experience challenges in communication, but unless they have qualifying disability, they will not be eligible for special education.

59. B: Although all of these factors can have a significant impact on a student, the content the student has learned has the greatest impact on the special education identification process. Students may come from many different cultures and have learned different topics and ideas. The special education identification process will look at a student's progress and how much they know about certain subjects compared with their peers. Answer A is incorrect because although the language a student speaks is important, it does not necessarily correspond to whether or not they should receive special education services. Answer C is incorrect because knowing where a student comes from can be helpful, but it does not influence identification. Answer D is incorrect because religion also does not influence identification.

60. C: There are many items included in an Individual Education Plan. These plans are designed to provide the school and other supporting personnel with enough information to offer the best possible educational experience and support for the student. Most plans include the date of implementation, signatures of the parent and student, health information, equipment the student will need in the classroom, and required personnel for the student. These plans also detail the additional time that the student requires in terms of support or tutoring, test results, goals, objectives, and desired outcomes. However, one item typically not listed in the IEP is the family's medical history or history of disabilities.

61. C: Vygotsky's zone of proximal development describes that a child benefits from exposure to knowledge that is only slightly beyond what they currently know. This implies that a student can benefit from receiving help from another child who is just slightly ahead in development. Peter is just starting long division, so having Joe help is fitting as his knowledge is slightly more advanced than Peter's. Joe may be able to explain long division in a fitting way that is accessible to Peter. Choice A is incorrect as Peter is not ready to do any fraction problems at this time. Choice B is incorrect as Peter does not need a reduction in work, he just needs some assistance. Choice D is incorrect because having the students work separately and then compare answers does not provide the direct scaffolding as in Vygotsky's theory.

62. A: Making labels in more than one language is not confusing to the children. Rather, it is supportive of their home language (if it is not English), and bilingual or multilingual labels send the message that writing comes in a variety of shapes and languages. A print-rich environment includes labels to identify objects and work areas, print that is at a child's eye level so it can be seen easily, and print that was created by the children themselves so that they can make the connection between print and their own work. That connection between individual creation and print is reinforced when the teacher models writing by preparing posters and other written materials in front of the children.

63. A: Letter-sound correspondence is the relationship between a spoken sound and the letters predictably used in English to transcribe them.

64. C: Guided practice involves students working together or with the assistance of the teacher. The purpose of implementing guided practice into the lesson plan, especially for students with disabilities, is to ensure that they understand the material by guiding them through it. Rather than just asking them to do the work by themselves right away, they can get some support from the teacher or their classmates. Answer A is incorrect because this would be an example of independent practice. Answer B is incorrect because this would be an example of teacher feedback rather than guided practice. Answer D is incorrect because teachers modeling the instruction would still be part of the instruction.

65. C: one-on-one stuttering therapy will benefit Erin, but keeping her in the same group is not the least restrictive setting for a student with a high IQ and good grades. Therefore, option A is incorrect.

Grouping Erin with other stutterers is more appropriate than grouping her with students who have delayed language development, but it is still not the least restrictive environment. A small group with other stutterers would be appropriate for pull-out speech therapy sessions but not for the whole school day. Therefore, option B is incorrect.

Because Erin has a high IQ and good grades, Donna is right to advocate for her placement in the general classroom. It is commonplace for students who stutter but have good academic achievement to be in the general classroom. Therefore, option C is correct.

Certainly stutterers have been embarrassed and even humiliated when they stuttered in front of large groups. However, this experience also occurs elsewhere in society, not just in school. Students who stutter are typically not segregated in school to protect them from embarrassment, which would still occur outside the classroom. Donna working individually with Erin would not constitute the least restrictive setting. It would also be impractical in terms of the use of Donna's time.

Frequent speech therapy sessions with Donna are indicated, along with having Erin spend the majority of the school day in the general classroom. Therefore, option D is incorrect.

66. A: The Americans with Disabilities Act. The ADA is a federal act prohibiting discrimination based on disability in the areas of employment, state and local government, public accommodations, commercial facilities, transportation and telecommunications.

67. B: A class may not be available. If one were available, it might teach useful skills but it would not be the same as gaining real-life experience. Also, William will be attending college classes and working part-time, so enrolling in another class on top of these commitments could overload his schedule. Therefore option A is incorrect.

Since William is proficient with computers, referring him to a website is a natural choice. The TASH website, for example, has a link to its Bridge Network, a free resource network that provides access to a database of contact information incorporating many needs of persons with disabilities. It includes resources for transitions from school to adult life, self-determination, and community living, among many others. Telling William about a website like this would enable him to locate resources on his own and avail himself of the support he needs to make this transition. Therefore option B is correct.

Advising William to try living on his own with a roommate with no previous such experience would provide him with no transition. Being autistic and spending a lot of time with computers, William may not have the best social skills for living with a roommate. Since he is interested in doing this but feels unsure how to go about it, he should not just attempt it without any preparation. He is less likely to experience success that way. Therefore option C is incorrect.

William could feasibly choose to stay at home while he attends classes and works. In many ways it would be easier than making a change. However, since he is interested in independent living, continuing to live at home would be a lack of progress. It would be better to encourage him to pursue his interest in progress and offer him sources of support and information to accomplish his objective. Therefore option D is incorrect.

68. A: Read all answers; mark out any that are illogical. Next 'plug in' the remaining words and mark out those that are grammatically incorrect or do not sound right. Finally, think about context clues. Maze and Cloze tests are related. In a Cloze test, the reader uses context clues and familiar vocabulary to decide which words have been left out of a text. A Maze test supplies a number of possible answers and the reader must select the correct one. Possible answers can be syntactically possible but illogical, syntactically impossible but semantically plausible and both illogical and grammatically impossible.

69. C: In order to understand why student behaviors have increased or declined, it is important to collect data before making major changes. Providing support to a student one on one is a significant change to the instruction that the student receives, so it should not be implemented until data have been collected on the student. These data might include what times of the day these behaviors arise or what kind of interactions may be involved with certain behaviors. Answer A is incorrect because the behavior may simply be a short-term situation in which the student does not display them consistently. Answer B is incorrect because although it may be a good thing to discuss at the annual IEP meeting, these do not always fall at the same time that changes need to be implemented. Answer D is incorrect because student suspensions do not necessarily dictate the level of support that a student receives in a class.

70. B: Specific learning disability is a disorder that affects a person's ability to listen, think, speak, read, write, spell, or do math. Auditory processing disorder affects a person's ability to listen. Answer A is incorrect because speech or language impairment is its own category of disability. Answers C and D are incorrect because each of these falls under other disability categories and not specific learning disability.

71. A: Although small-group pull-outs can provide opportunities for all of these choices, allowing these students to access their IEP accommodations is most important. These accommodations may include a quiet setting to learn, having texts read to them, or being retaught certain concepts. At the high school level, it is important to provide these accommodations to students so they can access as much of the general education curriculum as possible. Answer B is incorrect because students should be allowed to ask questions in any instructional setting, not just pull-outs. Answer C is incorrect because reducing teacher workload is not an instructional benefit. The purpose of separation is to improve student learning, not solely to make teaching easier. Answer D is incorrect because extra practice in reading, writing, or math is a secondary benefit. It may happen, but only if it aligns with the IEP goals.

72. C: Although each student may respond differently to challenging tasks, many students with ADHD will shut down if a task becomes too difficult. It is important to understand and recognize what the student is able to accomplish before challenging them. It can be embarrassing or cause anxiety for students who are unable to fulfill the challenge of the teacher. Answer A is incorrect because offering choices to the students allows them to feel like they are a part of the decision making. Answer B is incorrect because hands-on learning activities allow students to get up and move around. Answer D is incorrect because repeating the instructions often ensures that each student hears what is expected and does not forget.

73. A: Observer/informant behavior rating scales are the most appropriate for second-grade students. Answers B and D are incorrect because self-report scales tend to be more beneficial for older students who can accurately report their behavioral concerns. Answer C is incorrect because peer scales are rarely used, and they can present confidentiality concerns.

74. C: The Family Educational Rights and Privacy Act of 1974 protects student records. Under this legislation, parents (and eligible students once rights transfer at age 18 or upon attendance at a postsecondary institution) have the right to inspect and review the student's education records, and schools generally may not disclose these records to others without written consent, except in specific circumstances allowed by law (e.g., to school officials with a legitimate educational interest). Additionally, students have the opportunity to review their academic records and if necessary, make amendments in the instance of incorrect information. Information pertaining to the students' social security number, grades, grade point average, and academic performance are protected by this legislation, as well as information about behavioral issues such as suspensions, academic dishonesty, and probation.

75. A: Although the results of standardized assessments can be valuable tools, it is difficult to monitor the progress of the students when these tests are taken infrequently. It is best to monitor student growth frequently in order to determine if new interventions need to be put in place. When relying on tests that are only taken once or twice per year, it can be difficult to monitor progress. Answer B is incorrect because curriculum-based assessments can be given to students at any time to chart their progress. Answer C is incorrect because classroom observations can be beneficial for evaluating students with behavior goals. Answer D is incorrect because classroom grades can help to determine which subjects a student may struggle with.

76. C: While many laws are based on ethics, not all laws are ethical. Examples of what most would consider unethical laws include the Jim Crow laws in the United States that restricted the civil rights of black people or laws such as those imposed in Nazi Germany that permitted taking the lives and property of Jews. Answer A is correct in that laws are written, concrete, and enacted by people of authority. Answer B is correct in that ethics are a personal code enforced by a person's own conscience. Answer D is correct in that society transfers many of its ethics into laws to codify them.

77. C: The physical environment of a classroom is very important to effective learning. Classrooms that are bare will promote a cold, institutional feeling. This may inhibit learning. On the other hand, classrooms cluttered with information and posters may be too overwhelming for students and thus be counterproductive. In addition to ensuring that posters with appropriate content and an appropriate amount of information are used to decorate a room, proper lighting is also essential for creating an effective learning environment. Adequate lighting should be used to maintain attention and to prevent a dark environment where students and the teacher become sleepy during the day. This is especially important after lunch. If a classroom does not have enough lighting, the teacher can use lamps to increase the brightness of a room.

78. C: Engaging with a student through argument, negotiation, or appeal may prove to be the least effective strategy because it will likely make the behavior escalate. Many students are simply trying to get attention, and if they are given the attention they seek, they are going to make matters worse. Furthermore, it is inappropriate to negotiate or engage with a student openly in a class with other students because it could embarrass the student or perhaps even make it seem like they are getting special privledge over the other students. It would be a better option to remain calm and possibly seek some assistance if needed. Answer A is incorrect because ignoring her behavior may cause her to stop eventually, since she is not getting what she wants. Answer B is incorrect because calling for backup can be a great strategy, especially if there are safety concerns. Answer D is incorrect because removing her from class also might be the best option if the other students are being disturbed.

79. D: A 1998 survey by the National Association of County and City Health Officials (NACCHO) found that 13 states were centralized, 26 states were decentralized, and 11 states had mixed authority. All states do not have centralized organizational structures. Therefore, option A is incorrect.

All states are not decentralized. Therefore, option B is incorrect.

All states do not have mixed or shared authority between the state and the local health department. Therefore, option C is incorrect.

As shown in the survey cited above, some states are centralized, some are decentralized, and some share authority between the state and the local agencies. Therefore, option D is correct.

80. B: Although all of these choices could be potential conflicts in the co-teaching model, disagreeing on strategies is likely the greatest disadvantage. When teachers collaborate to teach a class, the general education teacher and special education teacher may have different approaches to certain topics and tasks. This may lead to some conflicts about the instructional strategies or how some of the students learn best. Answer A is incorrect because typically co-teaching will involve one teacher teaching more than the other. Answer C is incorrect because it is best to collaborate in subjects that teachers are familiar with in order to provide students with the best possible instruction. Answer D is incorrect because even if one teacher does not have as much experience, it is still possible to collaborate and learn from one another.

81. B: Although it may be difficult to plan when she will be absent from school, it would be beneficial to Cheyenne to have someone such as her case manager support her in this task. Making up work on a regular basis can be difficult to do for anyone, especially an eighth grader with a disability. The case manager can help Cheyenne come up with a plan for working with her teachers and getting her assignments in. Answer A is incorrect because although it may be helpful to have Cheyenne talk to her teachers, it may be an overwhelming task. Answer C is incorrect because coming in before school might be helpful but only if it is arranged in advance with her teachers. Answer D is incorrect because giving her a deadline may overwhelm her and make it difficult for her to complete any of her work.

82. D: When teaching a science lesson to a group of third-grade students, it is important to incorporate hands-on learning activities. Learning centers can provide opportunities for these students to do activities and learn about different topics. Learning centers are most appropriate for younger students, such as a group of third graders. Answer A is incorrect because reciprocal teaching would be most appropriate for older students who are capable of teaching each other rather than younger students. Answer B is incorrect because Socratic questioning would be most appropriate for higher level questioning based on thoughtful dialogue between the teacher and student and is a skill that third graders likely would not have. Answer C is incorrect because direct instruction may be more appropriate for a more abstract topic such as reading or math, as it does not promote hands-on exploration and investigation.

83. B: Learning to learn is one of the most valuable skills or learning strategies for the real-world environment. It helps students understand how they learn, check their own progress, and adjust their strategies. When teachers lecture, students are often taught facts but are not taught how to incorporate the facts into real life situations. Using the strategy of learning to learn teaches students how to solve problems and think critically. Additionally, when this method is combined with group learning, students learn how to interact with others in a team environment, which enhances leadership skills. While repetition and memorization are useful strategies for learning, learning to learn aids in implementing the strategies that work for the student and the student's specific situation.

84. B: Although all these choices may be helpful for Jimmy, it would be most appropriate for Jimmy's teachers to attempt some accommodations in the classroom. The first step in the prereferral process for special education is to provide additional supports for students inside the general education classroom. If this support is unsuccessful, then it may be a good idea to seek additional support and refer to the special education team. Answer A is incorrect because it is important to attempt interventions to determine how a student would respond before referring to special education. Answer C is incorrect because although a tutor may be helpful for Jimmy, it is best to first try some accommodations to see if those are successful. Answer D is incorrect because it may not be appropriate to offer to work with Jimmy after school.

85. D: Multilevel instructional practices can be used in various grouping arrangements, including whole class (A), small group (B), and paired (C) contexts; no one of these is better than the others. When arrangements other than whole class instruction are used, the smaller groups of students are typically still mixed in character rather than being homogeneous. Multilevel instruction is based on the principle that all students have a chance to access suitable instruction and to get support from their teachers and classmates.

86. A: Are results-oriented, includes post-school activities, vocational education, employment support, adult services and considers the individual's strengths, preferences and interests. Additional activities that compose Secondary Transition are instruction, related services, community experiences, the development of employment and other post-school adult living objectives and, if appropriate, acquisition of daily living skills and functional vocational evaluation.

87. A: Several aspects of this prompt are important in understanding the best approach. It is common for students at this age to have trouble staying seated and focused for long periods of time. Therefore, all approaches should be based on the assumption that the child is not necessarily abnormal until the behavior becomes patterned and debilitative despite creative classroom strategies. The student is not only neglecting his own work but keeping others from focusing as well. Alternating physical activity and schoolwork will give the boy breaks to release physical energy and help "ground" himself for the work at hand. He may also feel more able to complete the work if it is broken down into smaller, more manageable segments.

88. D: TerraNova is an example of a standardized test rather than a curriculum-based assessment. Curriculum-based assessments are designed to monitor the progress of students regularly, whereas standardized tests are given annually or semiannually to compare students to a norm. It is difficult to measure the progress of students on their IEP goals if they aren't monitored frequently. Answer A is incorrect because DIBELS is a common curriculum-based assessment that measures a student's abilities in reading. Answer B is incorrect because AIMSweb produces many curriculum-based assessment probes in the areas of reading, writing, and math. Answer C is incorrect because EasyCBM also assesses a student using curriculum-based assessment probes in many subjects.

89. B: Asking students to create a play about the story as the teacher reads aloud would be the most effective strategy. This activity grounds the students in the story action as it is occurring. Acting it out ensures understanding; otherwise, the students will most likely stop the teacher and ask for clarification. Furthermore, by acting it out, students are incorporating understanding physically. They will be more likely to retain the story and be able to comprehend the meanings incorporated in it.

90. A: When teaching students about study skills and how to use them, it is important to assist them in developing some methods that will work for them. Answer B is incorrect because independent practice would be difficult for students who are struggling to come up with ideas. Answer C is incorrect because developing a portfolio likely would be too much of a task to take on. Answer D is incorrect because although it may be beneficial, having a group discussion with the teacher's input is likely more beneficial in helping students develop successful study skills.

91. B: Students with developmental disabilities do not have a separate category and will likely fall under a different disability category according to IDEA. Developmental delay is considered a category for students who are ages three to nine, but this is not officially considered a developmental disability. It is important to understand the different disability categories in order to determine which category best fits the needs of a particular student. Answer a is incorrect because the multiple disabilities category is used for students who are impacted by more than one disability. Answer c is incorrect because the "intellectual disability" category would typically include students with developmental disabilities. Answer d is incorrect because the orthopedic impairment category meets the needs of students with physical disabilities.

92. B: This student has learned to perform the skills at home but has not generalized them to other settings. It is superfluous to reteach him the skills (A) because he has demonstrated their acquisition at home. Teaching skill maintenance (C) is unnecessary because the parents report he has performed the skills for years, so he has achieved maintenance but not generalization. Teaching skill discrimination (D) does not apply to this example as there was no mention of the student having any problems separating one skill or skill set from another or applying skills to the wrong tasks.

93. B: Because these two students come from a different culture, the two girls' behavior may be a result of differing cultural expectations instead of deliberate cheating. Given their backgrounds, Ms. George should be cognizant of these cultural differences and avoid penalizing them for their behavior. Punishing what is normal to them will only confuse them, so option A is incorrect. Since individual work is important in school settings, the teacher should work to properly explain classroom expectations in a culturally sensitive manner, so choice B is correct. The teacher could also consider assigning more group work, which the students may be more comfortable with.

Separating the girls would not be the best first action, as this could be seen as a punishment and make it harder for them to adapt to the new school setting. Due to their similar cultural backgrounds, the students are likely more comfortable working with each other, and separating them could lead to greater discomfort in the classroom.

Reporting the girls to the principal is punitive and unnecessary in this situation, so choice D is incorrect.

94. B: For students with specific learning disabilities, achievement tests are beneficial in gathering information about where the student may be deficient. Achievement tests such as the Wechsler Individual Achievement Test correspond with the categories associated with specific learning disabilities. This information is valuable in assessment of where students need improvement and potential strategies for instruction. Answer A is incorrect because this kind of assessment would be more appropriate for a younger student who is new to school. Answer C is incorrect because this assessment is typically used for those students who are at least 16 years old. Answer D is incorrect because this kind of assessment is an intelligence test rather than an achievement test.

95. D: To integrate Stewart into a classroom with no other wheelchairs, personnel should make sure that the room is wheelchair-accessible and that Stewart can navigate in the room. They should also instruct the other students how to avoid such things as tripping over footrests, accidentally kicking Stewart, bumping into his chair, getting their feet run over, blocking Stewart's path, and so forth. As long as accommodations are made in terms of the room's physical arrangement and everybody learns how to behave around a wheelchair, Stewart can be integrated into the classroom. Therefore, option D is correct.

To advise against the placement goes against the policy of inclusion. A student in a wheelchair has the right to be integrated into the general education classroom if he has the ability to participate in the educational activities of that class. Therefore, option A is incorrect.

Transferring Stewart from his wheelchair to a regular student desk and back again is unrealistic and impractical. It would require help, which might not be available. It would also be more restrictive. Staying in his wheelchair, Stewart has mobility in and out of the classroom, but if he cannot transfer between the wheelchair and another chair on his own, he will be dependent on somebody else to help him. Therefore, option B is incorrect.

Limiting Stewart's placement to only classes with other students in wheelchairs is not the least restrictive environment. Additionally, such a class may not be available. Or, even if there are other classes with students in wheelchairs, those classes may not be the most appropriate to Stewart's educational needs. Therefore, option C is incorrect.

96. C: What is true is not that teachers should spend less time or only their own time for professional development, but that teachers should actually spend more time—at least 20% of their work time—in professional study and collaborative work. Professional development is an essential part of teaching, and it is, therefore, legitimate to provide professional development opportunities during work time. Furthermore, it is also reasonable to expect teachers to incorporate continuous learning for themselves during the school day. Option A is what some critics of time spent on professional development say, but it shows a lack of understanding of the complexity and needs of the classroom teacher. Option B is also a common comment of critics of the educational system, but this criticism does not exhibit an understanding of the changes in education that require teachers to need education themselves in order to keep up. Option D is another common complaint from people who resent teachers being out of the classroom for professional development. Such complaints show a lack of understanding about the need for extensive, continuous professional development and a failure to recognize that time restraints might require taking teachers out of the classroom to accommodate the requirement.

97. B: Contacting the mother to see if Aaron missed his medication today would determine if his behavior was because of this, which is likely. Therefore, option B is correct.

Knowing that this student's mother has a history of sometimes having difficulty giving her son his medication, Mr. Love should act based on this information. Asking the doctor to raise the dosage would be inappropriate. Therefore, option A is incorrect.

Asking the principal to move Aaron to another class is not warranted under these circumstances. Since he does not usually display today's behavior in class, it is not likely due to his being in a class that does not meet his needs. Therefore, option C is incorrect.

Asking the doctor to consider a different drug is not indicated in this case. First Mr. Love needs to find out if Aaron received his medication today. Since today's behavior is atypical, there is no ongoing indication that his medication is ineffective. Since his mother sometimes misses giving Aaron his medication, this is the first possibility to investigate. Therefore, option D is incorrect.

98. B: It helps students to stick to a task if the task is made more fun by adding novelty to it through games or personal interest materials. For students who have difficulty staying with and completing routine tasks, the teacher can employ certain strategies that will encourage the child to stick with the work. One way is to explain to the students about the importance of remaining on-task and monitoring oneself. Another way is to eliminate any part of the routine that really isn't necessary, such as copying sentences. Still another way is to break up the task into smaller time commitments. In this way, the student doesn't get too bored before being allowed to go to something else, but they are nonetheless required to come back in a timely manner to finish.

99. C: Parents at the elementary school level must be updated on their child's progress on the IEP at least as often as they are provided report cards, which usually occurs each quarter. Answer A is incorrect because parents must be notified more frequently than once a year on the progress their child is making. Answer B is incorrect because weekly progress reports would be too frequent and not always provide the best data. Answer D is incorrect because being updated just at the beginning and end of the year is not sufficient enough.

100. B: One of the main purposes of IDEA in 2004 was to protect the rights of individuals with disabilities and their families. These laws allowed for parents to be more involved in the special education process and understand and be involved each step of the way. This was important in ensuring that the decisions made were by members of the team rather than just the school. Answer a is incorrect because IDEA emphasizes educating students with disabilities in the least restrictive environment rather than creating separate schools exclusively for them. Answer c is incorrect because, although IDEA gives students with disabilities additional procedural protections when expulsion is considered, it does not provide blanket immunity from expulsion; they still may be expelled in some circumstances. Answer d is incorrect because although IDEA may have caused many school districts to implement new programming, it did not specifically call for it.

Mometrix
TEST PREPARATION

STAAR

Test Prep Guide Grade 6 Reading Language Arts